Beautifully Bipolar:
An Inspiring Look Into Mental Illness

Erin Callinan

Published by Erin Callinan

Second Edition
Copyright © 2016 Peace of My Mind, LLC
All rights reserved

Cover Design by Erin Callinan

Cover image © 2013 Erin Callinan

ISBN - 10: 0-9890363-2-4
ISBN-13: 978-0-9890363-2-0

DEDICATION

To my parents Mike and Pril, and my brother Adam, you are
the light of my life. There are not enough words in this
world to express the amount of respect and gratitude I have
for each of you. Thank you for showering me with
unconditional love. You have offered me continuous
support and encouraged me to stand up tall with my head
held high. You are the most beautiful people I know.

CONTENTS

ACKNOWLEDGMENTS

Many thanks to the Bonnesens, Strombergs, Nordans, Callinans, Reileys, Campbells, Grandpa Fred, Grandma Jane, Grandma Pat and Papa Lee. Thank you for giving me the courage to share my journey with others. You all have been my rock and I love you so much.

To Kelsey Knight, Kerry Tealdi, Meghan Orrill, Stephanie and Erik Gerharter, Jenny Hendrickson, Joey Gossman, and Matt Warren, this book wouldn't be possible without each of you. Thank you for holding my hand through the shadows and reminding me how to smile.

To my mentor and eternal life coach, Dr. Elizabeth Caspian, This one's for you…

1 THIS IS BULLSHIT

Journal

September 6th, 2001
Senior Year of High School

I don't know why I have to be this way. Maybe this is why I began cutting myself. I'm not really sure why I do it, but I know that I always feel better afterwards. Why do I have to be fucked up in the head?

And even worse is that there is not a single person around me who knows what it feels like. Everyone continues to say that they're "scared for me" and I think that pisses me off more than anything. What does that even mean?

So now I have to live with this title forever, like it's some kind of fucking dog tag hanging around my neck. Is everything going to be "because she's bipolar?" What happens if there is an event in my life that causes me to struggle, something really serious that any normal person would have difficulty with? Something that I don't know how to get through and I cry and appear outwardly upset. Will it get pushed aside and dismissed because now we all know "she's bipolar"?

What happens when this fucked up disorder brings on serious depression or mania? Is anyone going to notice that I'm falling apart? Maybe they'll think I'm just making it up because I'm young and things like that happen to teenagers. Those are the toughest years right? That will drive me crazy.

What if I feel like I can do things different from other people my age, simply because I AM different? Maybe I do have talents, and really can do things others can't, because I have strengths and I am an individual. It's not because I'm having a manic episode and in my grandiosity thought I could do something wonderful.

I feel like the only reason that I might appear to be outgoing and charismatic, is because that's what the disease says happens when you're manic. Nobody will ever know what's going on in this destroyed head of mine, and I don't even want to tell them anymore, because they just blame it on the mania.

I abruptly shut my journal, only to realize that I've now lost myself. I am lost in my thoughts, I am lost in the eyes of others, and everything that Erin Callinan stands for is now re-labeled.

I have lost my individuality and it scares me, like waking up from a nightmare with sweat pouring from my brow and tears streaming down my face. Suddenly it strikes me. I am now a disorder. I am bipolar. I am not Erin Callinan, for she no longer exists. I am Erin Callinan, "That Girl Who's Bipolar."

So if I no longer carry this individuality and strength that I've flaunted throughout my seventeen years, then where am I in this world that once seemed so small? I am a weak member of the "mentally ill," being moved along in life like a herd of infected cattle. I no longer belong to the societal norm of a small town good girl, with married parents of twenty-five years, which alone makes me different.

I now limp with an unfamiliar type of independence, completely foreign to everything I know. Independent from happy surroundings of growing up with ease, I can no longer cross back over that bridge of normalcy. I am now different and set apart from those staring eyes.

They are the normal crowd that I was once a part of, yet the bridge between us is now a gaping hole, and there is nothing I can do to convince them that I still have a beating heart. I serve no importance to them, or anyone for that matter.

I live in a different world now. Not by choice, but because crazy girls like me are looked upon as a lost cause, and only useful for dinnertime gossip. This makes me physically ill and these gut wrenching realities make my head spin, until my insides are twisted and dizzy.

I am now to be stared at and talked about. Curious eyes peer at me and sink in like daggers through my soul. Everyone wants to know, "what happened to Erin Callinan?" Yet once they find out, hurtful stories fill their daily conversation with untruths and rumors.

Before all these empty feelings and dirty looks, laughter had surrounded me every day. I had a personality and a smile that I wasn't afraid to show. Yet, now I feel as though my face will literally crack if I try to smile. The muscles in my face are too tired. Too sad to move. What happened to giggling in the middle of the night, while my friends and I tried to hide the drunken slurs in our voices, so as to not wake my parents?

These days, those friends and memories are long gone, and my parents never sleep. They can't. They are responsible for watching my every move, ensuring I gulp down my new antipsychotic medications and refrain from killing myself. What kind of life is this? And how did I get here?

No longer am I a beautiful, young woman with a future full of happiness, that some envy with a half-hearted smile. You know the smile I'm talking about. One side of the mouth politely turned up, showing only a few side teeth, while the other side of the mouth drags bitterly behind tight lips.

As they attempt to fake being pleased that I have been blessed with many things, I know I'm standing before the shield of a forced smile. I know that when I turn away, they'll gripe under their breath that, "it's just not fair for people like her to get everything. She has no idea how hard life really is."

If they only knew the path my life would take. No, correction...the black hole that would suffocate me until holding my breath seemed to be a better option.

I'm barely seventeen years old, and breakdowns like this are supposed to be reserved for depressed drug addicts and insane homeless men. Yet here I am, an angry, bipolar ridden lunatic, with a ghostly complexion and hollow eyes.

God is punishing me. He is glaring down from Heaven with a lightning rod in hand. He hates me and I know it. But why? Did I take advantage of my loving family and friends, and overlook the possibility that it might not always be that way? Did I not take the time to show thanks to others? Should I have spent more time in the pew of a church, and less time at parties in parentless houses?

I have always been a believer in God, but I honestly don't know how I could put my faith in someone who would do this to me. He's ruining everything and I have no idea why.

I'm a good person. I'm smart, genuine and caring. What kind of sick God would turn ones' life into a dark and empty shell of something once filled with light? No God I've ever believed in could be this cruel. As I ponder how much I hate Him for doing this, my mind wanders to alternative motives.

Perhaps it wasn't God who did this to me. Maybe I was the one who caused this pain and suffering. What if I made some terrible mistake and my life has ended without me knowing it. I don't even know what realm of being I currently live in. Maybe this is why I no longer walk among the rest of the assured world.

I've heard of people who have died but for whatever reason, they don't cross over. It may have been some traumatic accident that they weren't prepared to endure, so their soul still lingers among the living. Could this be my Purgatory?

Maybe hell has already saved a spot for me, and the devil has taken my empty soul to fill it with. But my hell is worse than the usual sweltering heat and pitchforks; it's a living hell. I must walk among this earth half alive, with just enough blood to keep my lips from turning blue.

Yet everything else that defines me as a person is dead. I am a walking shell of a girl who once saw the beauty in life, and tried hard to grace others with the overflowing love she had received throughout her days. Now, my life is colorless and disapproving glares follow me like imaginary friends. It's like I can feel strangers breathing down my back as I walk by them. Can they tell I'm bipolar, and is that why they're staring?

Am I wearing my hatred for life on my face, out in the open for everyone to see? Do I even know them? Do they think I look disheveled and empty hearted compared to my normal put together self? Maybe they knew Erin Callinan…back when she was alive.

With my usual glazed over, blank expression, I stare back at them. I feel as though if I don't consciously remember to blink, my eyes will literally seal over, and only the water from my tears will pry them open again to see the life I once had.

2 BIPOLAR IS JUST A WORD; IT IS NOT WHO I AM

Here I am, Erin Callinan, twelve years later, reflecting on my temporary visit to what I like to call the "hot spot for crazies." This was my personal hell. One I thought the devil kept solely for bipolar people like me.

At twenty nine years old, I am a college graduate and successfully engaged in a career path that I love. I've made it, and you can too. However, I know the path from there to here is no easy feat. It takes time and it takes courage. For me...it took a whole lot of anger.

I don't recall ever selecting the MENTALLY ILL box when I completed the "What Do You Want to Be When You Grow Up" test when I was in 7th grade. So like many others, I wasn't prepared for this type of diagnosis. I wasn't ready to be labeled by a chart number, categorized as having a Serious Mental Illness, and considered a high-risk patient for insurance companies to pick up.

I worried that my future employers would uncover this secret sickness of mine, and tell me to pack my bags out of fear that I might catapult myself out the window, or explode like a loose cannon when they were least expecting it. I certainly did not sign up for this kind of life.

I was SO angry. Like the type of anger that makes the veins in your eyes pulsate. I was angry that I had to care about something that didn't previously affect me. Out of sight, out of mind.

I was angry that I wasn't strong enough to fight it. I felt that if I had enough courage, channeled my inner badass, and turned on my heavy, sometimes problematic stubbornness, I could conquer bipolar disorder. I could win.

I could take it down with one fell swoop, and smear that mood disorder into the ground. I'd humiliate it and stomp on its limbs, just as it had done to me. I'd gloat that I'd fallen victim to nothing. How did I see through the red with hopes that other colors of the rainbow actually existed?

Well…I got pissed, yelled, screamed and cried. Curse words flew out of my mouth as if their sour and vile taste made me physically ill. Because there it was. Anger. It was overbearing, unjustified and relentless. It didn't give a damn that it was capsizing the life I once felt I had control of.

Unfortunately for me, it wouldn't leave me until I'd first given anger the stage to be heard. Front and center, loud and clear. With cocky steps and its head held high, anger paraded around in my mind in an annoyingly proud and boastful way. It craved to remain in the spotlight…that is, until I killed the lights and unplugged the speakers.

How long was I going to allow anger to envelop the stage and suck the energy from my already exhausted body and mind? I had to learn not to let it stand between me and my recovery.

The longer I allowed it to take residency within me, the further away I was from finding stability, acceptance, and happiness. I provided myself a somewhat limited amount of time to feel and express all of the emotions I experienced, and acknowledged that anger was a part of my healing.

Letting go of my anger has allowed me to live a life in which I can celebrate my past because it's led me to find purpose in my present. I know I'm strong enough to endure and overcome anger should it make another attempt to take center stage. This time, I'm the one holding the microphone.

As I sit here years down the road, I find that the words of my life story flow out of me like a wave far out in the ocean dying to meet the shore. I now wake up in the morning without the grogginess of sadness, or the bitterness of the world around me.

Believe it or not, there *is* color in the world. The flowers have their smell back and the breeze is once again refreshing. The charcoal grey view of my dull surroundings has long since disappeared. Today I look back and recapture the broken thoughts and feelings of a seventeen year old train wreck. I can still hear the pain in my voice and the rambling in my head as I once tearfully scribbled in black ink.

My journal was a safe haven, and it was the only way for me to feel as though my words would never come back to haunt me. No one could judge me, talk behind my back or give me that look like "thank God it's her and not me."

Best of all, my journal was a progressive capsule of honesty. It is filled with self-hatred, anger, mania, embarrassment, love, tears, depression, growth and understanding, all of which have helped me through the darkness.

I have taken word for word entries from my journal to include in this book, with hopes that I can inspire just one person who might also live within the dungeons of their journal. It's okay, I did it too. I now have a new desire for writing. I no longer must push my scattered thoughts into the dark depths of my sacred journal.

This time, I am not writing to myself...I am writing this book to you. This is a book I wish I could have read when I was diagnosed with bipolar disorder in 2001. It's for those of you who feel alienated in your own world of insanity, and who now experience little hope through the devastation of this disorder.

The desperate call for healing doesn't stop there; further, it spreads to family, friends, siblings and spouses. It doesn't just affect the life of someone who has been diagnosed. It touches every person within an arm's reach and potentially beyond. I hope that whichever person you may be, this book will open up doors to the lights beyond the darkness of mania and depression, to a place of serenity and inspiration.

This is for those of you who are tired of hearing robotic doctors, rambling from a medical text, telling you what mania *should feel like*. How the hell would they know? Have they actually taken anti-psychotic medication that literally puts them in a self induced stupor to keep them from hurting themselves or others?

Have they gone night after night, without a blink of sleep, because their mind is racing so fast, it's like reading a comic book backwards while sitting next to a speaker at a KISS concert?

Let's talk about depression, because I'm sure they know the crippling feeling of barely having the strength to get out of bed. If you lie there long enough, maybe the pain will just go away. I've tried that, and for whatever reason I kept breathing, and could not sink into the depths of nothingness like I wanted to.

Let's move on to how this disorder changes the way people view you. Filled with shame and anger, do they get to helplessly watch as someone they love walks away? From a safe distance others would say to me, "You need more than I can give you, and I just don't know what to do with you anymore." You couldn't compile a group of more hurtful words.

I need just what any other person needs. I need love and guidance and patience and support. Don't walk away from me, even though I may be difficult. I don't want this lifestyle anymore than you want it for me.

To add to the list of things that make you feel like a complete whack job, the only news reports on TV or in magazines that cover bipolar cases, are typically those in which the unstable, manic depressive woman just murdered her children, then hopped on a bus to New York, not knowing how she got there, while managing to spend a massive portion of her husband's retirement money.

How about the deranged college student who opens fire in the middle of a crammed lecture hall, taking several lives along with his own? What kind of light does it shine upon those of us who have bipolar disorder and don't want to be labeled among the psychopaths and child molesters?

To me, this unsettling comparison doesn't make sense. I am not some case study or a collection of medical terms, nor am I a disillusioned killer. So, what then? Is this what it's like to be bipolar, and that's all my future holds?

Is my true self summed up by black and white stripes behind metal bars, peering out from the porthole of a mental institution, debt collectors at my door, or bottles of prescription medication lining my night stand? No.

I am not willing to follow in the footsteps of how the media and society portray a person who suffers from bipolar disorder. So I am writing this book to show that the word "bipolar" is just that. It's a word. It does not define who you are, or who you will become.

I have accepted that bipolar disorder is a part of my life, and I strongly oppose allowing it to create my identity. I have finally come to the realization that I am not being punished by the Man upstairs for wrongful doings in my life.

There must be a greater explanation for this black hole of depression and rollercoaster of mania that has nothing to do with hell, failure or punishment. Lucky for us all...there is.

This is my story of how I was taken under by the rough seas of a mood disorder, and came out still swimming with all parts fully intact. No life preserver necessary. I may have lost a flipper or two; but come to find out; they don't make for good walking shoes anyway.

Long after I returned from this trek underwater, I discovered that *I* was my own life preserver. By the end of this book, I hope you will look over your shoulder and see that yours is right there strapped to your back. It has always been there, yet we often look elsewhere to find our floatation device. Often, we do not realize that no such life jacket is as buoyant as our own.

3 SPINNING THOUGHTS AND TWISTED RAMBLING

It's August of 2001, and the summer is at a close. Standing in my room, I attempted to pull the two opposite sides of my duffle bag as close together as humanly possible. Packing for trips was never a talent of mine.

I looked down at the black Nike bag that once seemed much larger only to realize I had lost the fight. The suitcase sadly bulged open while the zipper made its best attempt to hold its breath, keeping the bag together.

Looking as if I'd packed a three hundred pound man into a small black leotard, I removed the unnecessary clothing and settled for a lighter load. Better. Four days at Lake Powell does not require this type of gear anyway.

All I needed was a cold Corona in one hand and my tanning oil in the other. Growing up, I didn't have the privilege of soaking my feet in the salty ocean water, so the lake was the next best thing. It was the beach for us Arizona kids.

I remember thinking; *this is going to be amazing. An unsupervised co-ed sleepover at the Lake! This is what every seventeen year old girl wishes for. The boys, the beer, the bathing suits. Oh shit, I forgot about that part. This body of mine is in no condition for running around with less than one foot of cloth covering me. Hmmm...I'll just drink until these thighs look a little slimmer. I'll be better looking with every sip.*

My intellectual thoughts are put on hold by the sounds of Kara's car horn. In more of a skip than a walk, I headed out to the car and piled in along with my other four best friends. I had no idea that I would return from this trip as a completely different person. A person I didn't recognize, nor would anyone else.

Beach side and ready to party, I held up my drink along with 12 other guys and girls on our houseboat. We were ready to get the weekend started, and how better to do that than with a good 'ol drinking game?

Now this wasn't any drinking game. This one ensures that you are likely to throw up on your own shoes, make out with the person to your left, or break down crying only to confess your love to each and every person you know. And to be honest, I was fine with all of the above.

But as the hours went by, I started to feel uncomfortable. Not the kind of uncomfortable feeling you have when your shoes are too tight, or you're filled to the max on Thanksgiving dinner. My insides felt uncomfortable. My soul was uneasy.

Something inside of me felt unfamiliar and strange, and I sensed it wasn't going away. I felt anxiety like I'd never felt before. By the third day at the lake, something inside me still felt foreign. I would have given anything to be somewhere familiar and safe. My mind was spinning. I was scared and too embarrassed to tell my friends what was really going through my mind.

Once I came to the realization that whatever had taken over my body wasn't about to go away, I decided to take a step back. I took a break away from the drunken chaos of my friends to walk around on the beach by myself for a bit.

As I looked aimlessly around the lake and surrounding canyons, everything looked seemingly different. It felt different. It smelled different. I couldn't quite put my finger on it, but my surroundings looked strange. The moving water glistened in the sun in a way that made me nauseous, like looking through a kaleidoscope. The waves jumped around in a panicked manner that jumbled my brain just by looking at them.

As I reflected back on the last few days, I figured that maybe I drank too much on the boat the night before. Maybe I was dehydrated and hadn't been getting enough sleep. Now don't get me wrong. Growing up, I was the epitome of a child with a vivid imagination.

I basically created the word hypochondriac. There wasn't a condition or disease I didn't think I had. I just knew that a headache meant a brain tumor, and a stomach cramp meant pancreatic cancer.

So when I would describe a pain or fear of being sick, I knew that I could count on being told, "Erin, sweetie, you're fine. If your head hurts, just take some Tylenol and you'll feel better. Grab some water and let yourself relax. You know how you work yourself up about these things." Just as usual, my parents were right. I always felt better, and no, I did not have the tumor I had convinced myself of.

As I sat in the sand and continued to think about how I felt, I realized I hadn't slept the last two nights. I remembered lying down with my friends in sleeping bags beside me. We stayed up late, laughing at nonsense jokes and chatting about things that were only funny to us drunken kids.

But come to think of it, I wasn't drunk. I had stopped drinking so that I would start to feel better, yet I felt as though I were drunk. I had the same drunken energy they did, and was able to stay awake and keep up with their ramblings. Yet, their ramblings sent them off to sleep. Mine kept me awake.

I could recall every minute of the seven hours we slept on the floor of that houseboat. I could have told you who sneezed, which person got up at 5:15 am to go to the bathroom, and who had snored the loudest. It didn't dawn on me until then that although I was physically lying in a sleeping bag with my eyes closed and body still, I was not asleep. My mind was extremely awake and there was no turning it off.

So if I could actually remember lying still for two straight nights without feeling like I ever slept, shouldn't I have felt tired? I should have been absolutely exhausted. Right? I felt flighty, almost delusional to the point where I was on some type of drug that caused my vision to change, and took away any need for food or rest. I never felt tired, and I couldn't stop thinking, moving or talking.

As the pieces of my unusual thoughts and feelings muddled together, I became panicked. I stood up and brushed the sand from my legs and reached for my phone. I made a call to my mom and expressed my concerns. She also thought I was probably dehydrated and had ultimately worked myself "into a tizzy."

Ninety nine percent of the time, she was right and I was going to be fine. This time served as the one percent chance of her being wrong. Within twenty four hours of this phone conversation, I knew. I was going crazy. Fortunately, two of the guys we were with on the boat were leaving early, and I was able to catch a ride back to Flagstaff with them.

Within two minutes of shutting the front door of my house and dropping my bag on the kitchen floor, I found myself begging for comfort over my brothers open Bible. Something was wrong.

I was more than dehydrated and beyond tired. After another panicked phone call to my mom, she rushed home. Soon after, we were on our way to the Emergency Room. I don't know if my mom really knew the sickness I felt, but the worry that filled my eyes convinced her that this was no joke. I needed help and she could sense how afraid I was.

We spent the next few hours in the Emergency Room, and just as I feared, the doctor narrowed it down and told me that I was suffering from anxiety and dehydration. In a calm demeanor, the doctor replied, "You just need to slow down. You're burning the candle at both ends." If only that were true. I felt like I was skydiving with no parachute.

I so badly wanted the doctor to confirm the sickness in my stomach and the swirling confusion in my head with something more than that. I fell into a state of chaos and disorientation. My mom and dad had planned a trip out of the country, and whatever was happening to me, I did not want my parents to be thousands of miles away.

I knew there was something wrong. And I felt that it was only going to get worse. I remember closing my eyes and praying that when I opened them, my surroundings would look normal. By normal, I mean the same view I had seen for the last seventeen years.

The cars on the street, the surrounding trees, or shape of your own hands…you never think twice about them. Excluding minor changes, they look just as they did the last time you saw them. But for some reason, everything looked different and my hallucinations were dumbed down with my normal "over reaction."

I felt like I was in a toy land brushed over with a matte glaze. Like a train set that wraps around the Christmas tree, it appeared that nothing was life size. Leaves on trees looked polished and fake, and my sense of reality dwindled with every passing day.

I could see each and every little detail of plants as if I had super powers that nobody else had access to. My vision was so clear it made me nauseous, like I had suddenly activated parts of my brain that had never been used by another human.

I sat on the couch, un-showered and in a world of my own. I looked outside to see the rain dancing off the deck in my back yard, and asked my mom "Is the ground getting wet?" Kind of a no-brainer question, right? But at the time, nothing made sense to me and concepts didn't connect.

I could watch a television commercial and think it was a message sent through the TV, specifically for me. It carried some type of underlying meaning, and I could understand things that other people couldn't. My parents feared that normalcy might never return, because their singing, laughing daughter was nowhere in sight.

Completely unclear of where she might have gone, they knew that Erin was nowhere near this outward frame that suggested to have once been their daughter. They talked to my friends from the houseboat to see if something happened while I was there, but no one had answers. Each day became worse and worse, and after a trip to the ER, an eye doctor, and my primary care physician, we still had nothing.

Finally, I fell apart. Ideas and thoughts raced quickly through my head like a flipbook. Page after page, more pictures and words, over and over, expressions and lights. Pacing and moving and thinking and spinning. They raced. Faster and faster, lacking any sense or glimpse of reality.

Yet they continued, and I hated myself. I hated myself for allowing them to continue to taunt me. It was a complete array of absolute nonsense that filled my mind, and everything that came out of my mouth was just as ludicrous as my thoughts.

As I gave in to the insanity, I found my way to the family room and let my words confess my own hearts desires. I looked my mom straight in the eye, without tears or emotion and whispered the most devastating words a mother could hear. "If you don't get me help soon mom, I'm going to kill myself."

Tears dropped on the pages of the phone book as my mom flipped through the advertisements looking for a psychologist. She knew. She knew from the start that something was wrong, yet this was confirmation that I had reached the end of my rope.

I could only be a walking body of craziness for so long before the mania and misery would ultimately overtake me. Frantically searching for help, she randomly chose a psychologist from the phone book and within twenty minutes we were on our way to Dr. Reed's office.

I didn't know where I was going, or what it would be like, but sure enough I was going to see a shrink. How could my life have possibly come to this? Shit. I thought I was better than that hippie therapy, "tell me how you feel" crap.

4 THE LOONEY BIN

The sounds of waterfalls and wind chimes played from a stereo just over my shoulder and the feng shui of the place did seem to ease my nerves. But the many plants around the office reaffirmed my inability to see clearly. *What is with all the fake, plastic looking plants?* I thought.

I knew that was not how they really looked. I eagerly waited for my vision to return to normal because the longer things looked different, the more unsettled I became. My thoughts were all over the place, jumping from one side of my brain, and bouncing off the other.

I heard the door open, and I abruptly looked to my left and caught eyes with Dr. Reed. Just as I had seen in the movies, she sat in a big leather chair in front of me, while I crossed my legs on an earth-tone colored couch.

One of the first things I asked her was, "Can someone really go crazy? You know, like one day, something changes and they just go mad?" She tried not to be obvious about her annoyance with my question, and stared at me as if I was another dramatic teenager wasting her time.

My session with her didn't uncover any earth-shattering break through; however, she verified that I was suffering from anxiety. Dr. Reed assured me that my sporadic emotions and sensations would cease if I "remembered to breathe." She even gave me a blue rubber band to put on my wrist, so that every time I saw it I would do just that. Breathe.

She encouraged me to stop all of my extracurricular activities so I could focus on breathing and centering myself, free from outside distractions. Quit cheerleading and student council to take warm baths and read self help books? *Are you fucking kidding me?*

We would soon find out that anxiety and lack of oxygen was not the issue at hand. I was not dehydrated and I was not over reacting. I became ill, in every possible meaning of the word. A few days after my visit with Dr. Reed, my parents left for their vacation out of the country. Everyone was hoping I was headed uphill and would be feeling better, but just to be sure, I went to stay with my Aunt Liz and Uncle Van in Phoenix, AZ.

I was extremely close to Liz and Van and spent much of my growing up with them and their two kids, Chad and Logan. This was unlike any visit I'd ever had at their house. I thought I felt crazy when I arrived home from Lake Powell days earlier, but I was now soaring into full blown psychosis.

The worried look on Liz and Vans' faces validated that they were coming to the realization that I was not Erin. I was a lifeless stranger who knew nothing more than a four year old child. I could barely function, and whatever disease had a hold of me, it was not letting up.

I stared blankly when they spoke to me with a furrowed brow and empty eyes. I wandered around the house on my tip toes and muttered ramblings to myself.

The old Erin Callinan knew how to work a TV remote control. "ON" meant the TV would work, and "OFF" meant it didn't. My cousin Logan spent a solid 10 minutes explaining the basics to me as if I was from a foreign country that didn't have televisions. I yearned for comfort and normalcy.

Thankfully my brother Adam came down from vacationing in Seattle to spend the week with me. I needed him. Especially at night when I tried to sleep, which was the time of day filled with the most torture. My thoughts ran wild and my skin crawled with thoughts of death.

I talked constantly. Over and over, more words and thoughts, again and again. Adam would tell me to close my eyes and practice taking deep breaths. He assured me that everything would be okay.

Before long, I would hear him falling into a deep sleep, and only the sounds of my heartbeat reverberated in my head. Just like a child doesn't know how to tie their own shoes, I didn't know how to care for myself. I didn't know life from death or reality from fiction.

I wet the bed with my 19 year old brother lying next to me. Continuously. And Adam stayed with me. Frustrated with confusion, he searched to make sense of the situation. He wanted to help his little sister, he wanted her back. But Adam didn't know what was wrong with me, or why I acted the way I did.

I had no control of my thoughts, my body, my responses or my behaviors. This night continues to be the only recollection I have of him spending the week with me at Liz and Van's.

What happened that weekend at the Lake? What the hell was wrong with me? Was I raped and couldn't deal with the trauma so I just freaked out? Was I slipped some type of drug without my knowledge? Did I just totally fall off the deep end? Most importantly, was I ever coming back?

Here we go again, another trip to the emergency room. Only one day had passed since my parents left town and my condition had continued to decline. I remember walking into the front entrance of the ER and the woman behind the desk asking me my name. I had no response. I really didn't know who I was.

While at the emergency room, they hooked me up to all kinds of machines and left me staring up at the white ceiling while doctors discussed my condition with my family. Everything about the room looked so medical, so sterile. I knew it must have been some kind of lab where they were going to open up my head and dissect my brain.

I continued to wet the bed and feared that every beep I heard would indicate my last breathe. Fortunately, I stopped peeing for an amount of time long enough that they decided they weren't going to give me a catheter.

After doctor's consultations with my family and phone calls with my parents, I was being discharged. From this hospital at least. The place I was about to go would forever change my life.

Upon returning home to Liz and Van's, the last logical memory I had was lying naked, three inches underwater in the bath tub. My best friend Jenny from Flagstaff rushed down to Phoenix when she received the call that I was being "checked in."

My needs exceeded the services at the emergency room, and I had to be immediately moved to a behavioral health unit for further observation.

Jenny arrived at Liz and Van's and walked inside to hug me as tears filled her bright blue eyes. She took me by the hand and led me to the upstairs bathroom. Jenny was there to help prepare me for my "trip."

She undressed by helpless body, starting with my sweater and she gently put me in the bathtub. Being the seventeen year old girl that I was, you would think I could have at least undressed myself and saved some dignity by stepping into the tub with discretion. But the difference between the bathtub and the kitchen sink made no difference to me.

I remember lying naked in the tub thinking that I didn't need to breathe. Oxygen was no longer a necessity of mine. I could sink my head under water and the thought of coming up for air never dawned on me. But Jenny was there. She held up my head, and washed my body from my head to my toes. She spoke to me in such a soothing way, as if talking to a puppy.

After helping me from the bathtub to stand me upright, Jenny attempted to blow-dry my hair. I looked in the mirror as if I was looking at a stranger with frizzy hair and dark, empty eyes. After putting in enough effort to make me somewhat presentable to the world, she grabbed my bag of clothing and toiletries, and we were headed out.

It was August of 2001, and I was admitted to a psychiatric hospital in Phoenix, Arizona. After medical advice from my primary care physician, as well as those from the emergency room, Liz and Van sat by my side as they checked me in to a mental health facility. Wow. It was actually happening.

Within an hour, I sat hunched over and blankly stared at the light green hospital band on my wrist. Little did I know I would spend the next six days there...in the nut house. I closed my eyes and tried to remember how I got there. This was it, my life was over.

Something had happened to me that caused me to absolutely lose my mind. I was a pale, delirious, stranger with vacant eyes, dry lips and unkempt hair. I was now one of "them"...hospital gown and all.

As I sit here now and think about it, the decision to admit me must have been truly gut wrenching for Liz and Van. My parents weren't present, so my well-being was completely in their hands. It had only been 24 hours since my parents left the country, and they were in constant communication with Liz and Van.

They were frantic. Sick to their stomachs. A total sense of helplessness that I'm sure will never be removed from their memory. My parents had been scrambling to catch an immediate flight home and when they finally did, it was the next day. It must have been the worst flight of their life.

All they wanted was to be with their little girl, the one who left and no one knew why. Through tears, pain and confusion, my parents gave consent for Liz and Van to check me in to a psychiatric hospital. I needed too much care to stay with them at their house.

Upon arriving at the hospital, we walked into an open room filled with couches and magazines. From what I remember, there were a few other people in the waiting room. I wasn't sure whether they were the patients or the family, but I figured they wouldn't dare let one of us crazies out with the rest of the world. They must be family. Before long, I was called back by a behavioral health technician for my evaluation.

Now when you check into a mental hospital, you don't just go tromping in the front door and fess up that you're a mad man...lights are on and nobody's home. Just trying to get into this place was like entering a high security prison. It was intimidating to say the least.

Once you've received permission to get through the double paned glass porthole that cuts out a portion of the steel door that weighs no less than three thousand pounds, you may enter. The doors unlock only from behind the nurses' station or the front desk, and the noise they make when they do is one that will always haunt me.

The sound is like riding a roller coaster up to the highest point before speeding down the winding tracks, making everyone's head spin. You hear the click, click, click, as the rollercoaster approaches the climax of the ride, and then it stops for a brief moment. Then there's that one last CLICK right before it releases you through the air. *That's the click.*

It's loud and unnerving. The scraping of the doors metal pieces moving so quickly past each other in opposite directions creates a rumble deep down inside your belly. That is what the doors at the hospital sound like and I knew then that I was being caged up along with other crazy people like me.

Being that I was in a complete stupor, disillusioned and out of sorts, I wasn't much help with the intake questions. Apparently I was supposed to reply with some form of lucid response that would inform them of my name, age, place of residence etc. Yeah, good luck with that.

I was grateful to have Adam, Liz, Van and Jenny there with me. They were my voice. They were everything. And they did their best to help answer all of the nurses' questions. Yet some of the questions were so personal. They were the type that didn't typically come up at family dinners over flank steak and baked potatoes.

I remember being asked, "Have you ever used methamphetamine?" As if being asked if I brushed my teeth that morning, I nonchalantly shook my head yes.

They quickly responded with, "Have you used meth within the last week?" Thinking of how seriously they took my answer the first time, I figured this must be some kind of game and I'm obviously doing a great job. Clearly I was winning. "Yup." I mumbled back. Now, not only had I never even seen meth, I certainly had never used it.

My mind was racing unbelievably fast, and I couldn't tell the difference between my words and theirs, so I simply agreed with whatever they had to say. I was so confused. The next thing I knew, they removed my jewelry, shoelaces, hair tie and drawstring from my hooded sweatshirt. I was admitted into the hospital under the beautiful category of "suicide watch."

As I began my first day in the children's ward (I was still a minor) at the hospital, I had been without sleep for six or seven straight days. I didn't sleep at Lake Powell, I didn't sleep when I was back in Flagstaff, or when I went to Phoenix and stayed at Liz and Van's.

As I was about to spend my first night in the looney bin, my parents rushed off the plane as it landed in Phoenix and came directly to the hospital. They were informed that the doctors were going to try and stabilize me in order for me to sleep, and then they would explore a diagnosis.

Within the first two hours I was there, the word "bipolar" hung in the air like a kite on a breezy summer afternoon. I kept hearing it as if it were being mentioned from a conversation far, far away. The word was all around me. But who really knew what the hell that meant, nor anyone who had it? Certainly not me.

Four yellowed walls enclosed my new habitat. Looking around, there was two of everything. Two beds, two dressers, and two desks. Slightly confused, I didn't notice two of us in the room, but I learned that a roommate would soon be coming my way.

The walls had scratches and indentations of gang signs, devil horns, crucifixes and poetry. Even the windows were inscribed with the tormented thoughts of previous patients. I wondered how they did this. Considering I couldn't even have long fingernails, a hairbrush or shoelaces, I was curious to what extremes people went to get their thoughts and feelings etched into this haunting place.

The beds were less than appealing, unless plastic was considered a nice way to keep from having to wash the pillow cases regularly. The sheets felt like one ply toilet paper that lacked heat and comfort. This didn't really matter though, for sleep and I had not been the closest of friends lately.

I remember looking out of my bedroom window over the parking lot. All of the cars below seemed so small. They looked like toys with miniature people inside of them. I was looking out into a world that made no sense to me what so ever.

The two slats they called windows felt so confining and punitive. As if when you looked through them, they giggled back and reminded you that you weren't worth more than the tiny view they provided. I felt like I was in a dream. A dream that I couldn't control, explain, or scream loud enough to get out of.

5 FROM RESTRAINTS TO FRECKLES

I remember being strapped down. I remember the blue paste that swept my forehead as they attached the electronic magnets. I remember looking at the man with the bow tie and large nose. Apparently, the nurses were attempting to do an EEG (electroencephalogram) on me, but with little luck.

Three strangers stood above me, perched over and peering down like I was twenty feet below them. The doctor had on a black suit and a red bow tie, which only compounded the creepiness of the situation. His demeanor was cold and removed, as if he was going out of his way to do this work, and giving me commands like a dog.

When I wouldn't respond, I'd get that look that your parents give you when you've disappointed them. How was I to know what he wanted? I was so medicated; I couldn't even identify myself by my first name.

As a crew of nurses and technicians surrounded me, another male doctor leaned in beyond the others. He stretched out a yellow tape measure from the top of my head, directly across my face and down to my chin. *Are they measuring my head and body to fit the casket for my burial? Am I dead, and now the creep in the bow tie is preparing to put me in the ground?*

Several electrodes were pasted on my forehead and the multicolored wires draped across my face and chest. Beyond all the wires were those same rigid, removed, and unfamiliar faces. "Relax Erin. It's okay Erin. Be still Erin." They spoke to me in a way that made me panic. *What is happening? Why are they doing this to me? I feel scared! I feel unsafe! I have to get out of here!*

As I frantically tried to brush the wires from my face and the electrodes from my forehead, the blue paste that held them on painted my fingers. It was the color and consistency of blue Crest toothpaste. There was no emotional connection or compassion for the girl beneath the wires. I felt like I was starring in my very own Frankenstein movie, but when I wanted to scream out "CUT!" they tied me down.

As if I were some out-of-control convicted criminal, I was completely bound and restrained from any movement. They took some form of strap and individually tied my hands to the rails at my sides, while two of the technicians held my ankles to the corners of the bed.

Maybe it was because I was on suicide watch? No, that can't be. I had done nothing to indicate that I was going to harm them, or myself. It was about power and their ability and need to control me. I felt like an animal.

Why didn't they take the time to explain what was happening to me? Why couldn't they have told me step by step what they were going to do and why they were going to do it? I had no control of my body or how it was being handled. My confusion stemmed from psychosis and it was now compounded by the pace of everything around me. It all happened so fast, and yet it is one of my most vivid memories.

"She's not cooperating! We've got to keep her still. We've got to do this test! Erin! Erin! Don't fight it. Give her the shot!"

And they did. They released my ankles, rolled me over to one side, and yanked the back of my pants down until my entire backside was exposed.

It was as if I were an unruly four year old acting up in front of guests, and about to be humiliated and spanked bare assed in front of uncomfortable eyes. First I felt the needle, along came the sting, and then I don't remember. The next time I woke up, the machine was gone and my fingers were still dipped in blue Crest toothpaste. The painful bruise on my butt stayed with me for many days after.

I stood from my bed and walked into the bathroom. I remember looking down at my sickly self and not being able to recognize the person looking back at me. Turning to look in the mirror, I was a ghostly person with sunken eyes and dried out lips. My hair was greasy and frizzy, and stuck to portions of my head like I'd been on bed rest for days.

Is this real? I lifted up my white t-shirt to see the thin frame that barely had the energy to keep me upright. My ribs stuck out and my waist looked different. My belly button was different. I knew there were once two piercings in my navel, and now only empty holes remained. Who is this girl?

Continuing my focus in the mirror, I pulled down my blue shorts with white stripes that lined the sides. I held my shirt up underneath my chin, as my shorts sat on the floor hanging near my ankles.

Whose are these? I wore cotton underwear with decorative stripes that covered my entire butt. I looked like a child again, wearing my dad's t-shirt and my Monday through Sunday panties. I knew the clothing I was wearing did not belong to me, but I had no idea to whom they belonged. I turned from the mirror and walked in a zombie like fashion to the other side of the room.

I pulled open the dresser drawer only to find more piles of clothes that didn't belong to me. Running shorts, plain grey and white t-shirts and that damn underwear again. I didn't have a roommate yet, and the entirety of the situation brought on confusion. *Where are all of my clothes?*

I again turned to face the mirror which confirmed that I was in desperate need of some TLC. Nobody had been taking care of me. I smelled. The stench that surrounded me reflected someone who had been ill and holed up in a room for days. Everything smelled stale, as if it were seeping through the walls.

I moved toward the stand alone shower that was set back in the corner of the bathroom. It was tiled and barren, and the drain at the bottom carried residue of former psychos. I pulled the shower curtain over to one side, and turned the water knob to the left. Now you would assume that in a ward full of crazies, they would have made this whole shower situation a bit easier.

The shower stood tall, no bathtub or anything. The knobs and showerhead were placed directly in front of you when you pulled back the curtain. So when you turn the knob to turn the shower on, you were immediately blasted with water.

There I stood, dripping wet in my extra large white t-shirt, shorts nearing the ground and my 3rd grade cotton panties. This frustrating dilemma seemed to launch me back into the twilight zone, because my mind went blank. I don't know how long I stood there as water poured over me and the clothes I was wearing.

The next moment I recall is standing in the middle of the great room, where all of the other kids played. In the center, there were couches, tables, and cabinets that remained locked. It was a big open area where activities and group meetings were held. The door of every patient's room opened up to this great room. There I stood. Dripping and lifeless, hoping someone would help me. Instead, they all stared.

My parents later informed me that I had displayed this shower episode to the other patients several times before and came out wet and half naked. Hence the strange cotton panties, sports bras and t-shirts in my dresser. They were trying their best to keep me covered.

By the time it was my fourth day in the hospital, I had not spoken a single word. The other kids in the hospital literally didn't think I had the capability to speak.

One morning a boy about the age of 10 wanted to help me communicate with the group, so he handed over a coloring book and a set of crayons. He pointed to the blank underside of the coloring book cover, and told me to write down what I wanted to say. All I wrote was the letter I. Over and over again, "I, I, I, I, I" was all that I could get out.

There were group activities and therapy session all patients were required to attend. The program was based off a point system and you moved forward in your recovery each time you were placed at the next "level." The higher you climbed in levels, the closer you were to being discharged.

You would earn points by fulfilling daily activities and responsibilities. Each morning, we all had to meet in the great room to discuss what we were thankful for and identify our daily goal. For example, if I ate breakfast, made my bed and contributed during one support group, I could get four points for the day.

I don't think I earned a single point until at least my fourth day, because I never spoke. I couldn't contribute in group and I couldn't follow simple instructions. Being so heavily medicated limited my ability to participate in anything, and there are large spans of time during this hospital visit that I still don't remember at all. Spans of time are completely absent from my memory.

Occasionally all of us patients would be treated to a movie, and would huddle around a TV screen that was wheeled into the center of the room. However, a boy with quite the anger issue was persistent in walking around and violently kicking the sides of your chair, so these "freebie" activities were usually put to a halt.

My parents came to see me at every possible moment visiting hours would allow. When they did, I could recall them talking about Erin. Every time they would bring this person up, I would reply "She's gone." They would try and get clarification to discover what I was talking about. And I would repeat, "Erin's gone."

It confused me when they spoke of this girl. I didn't know this "Erin" that they talked about, but when they brought her up, I felt great sadness. But not nearly as much as the heart break my parents felt when I spoke this way.

As I began to stabilize on my medications after the first 4 days or so, I began to come back to reality. I was able to form sentences and make the connection between my physical body and my thoughts. "Coming down" from a manic episode and stabilizing after psychosis is quite a process. It's almost as if your entire brain is trying to re-program itself. Your mind has been injured and it needs time to slowly heal.

I can only compare it to the effects you experience after being put under. As the anesthesia wears off, you slowly begin to gain understanding of where you are, and who you are. I was able to realize that this "Erin" girl they spoke of was me.

As the grayness left my mind and I slowly re-entered reality, I remembered Abraham. I remembered him from my dreams. On the fifth day, my mom came to visit me and brought with her some mini boxes of cereal. Realizing she forgot to pair them with a plastic spoon, she went out to the main area and asked the charge nurse for one. The man replied, "what for?" and my mom responded, "I'm going to feed my daughter Erin, she said that she's hungry."

As if my mom had said she just resurrected a human body from six feet under, he replied, "Erin? She doesn't talk!" The perplexed look that swept his face affirmed his thinking that my ability to form sentences was clearly out of the question.

My mom knew the only condition he had seen me in was numb and disconnected. She smiled kindly and said, "Come with me, would you like to meet my daughter?" She knew that none of the doctors or nurses had had a real conversation with me. Well, at least not one that I participated in. The man agreed to meet me, and as I sat cross legged on my bed, they entered the room together.

From the moment he walked in, I felt a sense of calmness and serenity. He came to the side of my bed and said, "Hi Erin, it's nice to meet you." I remembered him, it was Abraham.

When I first entered the hospital they put me on a heavy regiment of medication to allow me to sleep and stabilize the chemical imbalance in my brain. I remembered lying in my tomblike bed wrapped up in white sheets and watching the shadows dance upon the wall.

At first it took me awhile to fall asleep, and I could see a nurse peering through the port hole in my door every few hours. But once I finally fell asleep, I slept for 26 hours straight. Somewhere during that time, Abraham came in to see me.

He was one of the nurses that would come and check on me in the middle of the night. I don't know if the purpose of the checks was to ensure I hadn't tried to tie the sheets together and strangle myself or to keep tabs on my delirious behaviors.

Yet Abraham actually opened the door one night and came into my room. He pulled up a wooden chair next to my bed and sat with me. He was an African American man with light cocoa skin. He had curly hair gelled closely to his head and his face danced with freckles.

Abraham took my hand between his and sat with me. His hands felt warm and surprisingly comforting. I could hear him speaking softly, but I don't recall what he was saying. It didn't really matter. All I knew was that he held my hand and spoke to me when no other nurse did. It was one of the few times I didn't feel afraid.

When Abraham came in with my mom to "meet me," I softly whispered, "I dreamt about you. You came into my room and held my hand. You talked with me." He smiled and shook his head in agreement. His face turned toward my mom and a look of utter shock came over him.

How could she have possibly remembered those moments we shared? He looked as if he wanted to say, "She's come back to life!" I took another glimpse at those freckles and thanked him as he left the room.

On the sixth day, I was able to leave the hospital. My family came to pick me up and I went back to my Aunt Liz and Uncle Vans house. It felt like I had been in a major car accident and had to relearn everything.

I wasn't sure how to unlock the car door, and it took me a while to respond when someone was talking to me. Remembering how and when to brush my teeth didn't come naturally, and I would have never thought to eat anything if someone didn't make me. I didn't look forward to things or people, as I had difficulty remembering who I was in my former life.

I was still very heavily medicated and connecting to any feelings or emotions was challenging. After discharge they had me taking 1500 mg of Depakote and 22.5 mg of Zyprexa. For those of you who have taken these medications before know this is a high enough dose to practically sedate a horse.

I felt injured, with only enough energy to keep me breathing. A few friends sent cards during this time, and some even offered to come by after I was released from the hospital and went home to Flagstaff. But I didn't want to see anyone. I was ashamed, vulnerable and broken.

For the last two weeks I was convinced I was veering down the winding streets of hell, and now that I wasn't, it meant I had to try again. I felt as though I had to crawl back up the sides of the cliffs to get back to normal life at the top. I barely knew what normal was.

Now back in Flagstaff I had to continue recovering from the trauma both my mind and body had been through. I was confused and I was angry. Three days after being released from spending a week in a psychiatric hospital, I started my senior year of high school.

Journal

September 9th, 2001

I have never felt more dead my in entire life. While I was in the hospital, it was like I was dying and my whole life was put in perspective. I did not know what was happening, or why it was happening.

It honestly felt like I had died and never made it to heaven. So I was stuck in between, and all I had to do was look at my life and every single thing I have done wrong that could have led to this. You only have one chance at life, and it felt like I was looking upon the life I used to live, almost soaring above it. I must have done something to deserve this.

I'm sure everyone thinks about killing themselves at one time or another. But now I'm at the point where I actually want to die. Sometimes I slap myself across the face as hard as I can, just to make sure I'm actually alive.

I have no feeling, it never hurts. I never cry, or have emotions. I don't care at all. I don't care about the people around me, I don't care about myself and I don't care about living. In the hospital, it felt like everyone else around me was dead, nothing felt real. I stopped eating, I stopped showering, and I stopped everything to pretend I stopped living.

I wanted to die, but I didn't know how to let go enough to end it, and that's why I felt stuck in the middle. I'm not sure how much different I feel now.

6 THE GIFT

Being out of the hospital was incredibly nice, as I was now at home surrounded by family. My mom and dad were absolute miracles for me. They had the patience of saints, yet being around me was anything but angelic.

How they managed to keep their hearts in the right spot, while I spewed vile hatred for life is beyond me. The turmoil I went through was hard to recover from. It's similar to the severity of a hangover, based off how much alcohol you've consumed. The more you consume, the worse you're going to feel afterwards.

The level of mania I experienced and the deregulation of chemicals in my brain caused a sort of "hangover" period for me. The higher my head went, the lower my heart went, and I experienced a great deal of depression once I was released from the hospital. I hated even stepping outside.

People are staring. I know they are. They can sense that I am crazy. Why are they looking at me like that? It must be obvious that I was just in a mental hospital. I felt as though every person that walked by me was judging me and could read the bipolar diagnosis written across my face.

I felt in my heart that everyone I encountered knew I had a mental illness. But did I really suffer from bipolar disorder? The doctors from the hospital sure seemed to think so. I distinctly remember the haunting way I felt when they talked about me as a "manic depressive." Like it was my name tag secured tightly to my shirt letting everyone know my identity.

The drug tests I took verified there were no drugs in my system. *But how could that be? Are they sure I wasn't slipped something? I just freaked out and went crazy? How could God have seriously put me through this? And now I have to face my peers?*

The last thing I wanted to be was talked about. "Did you hear Erin freaked out and they locked her up in a psych ward?" or "Did you hear Erin was raped or something so she tried to kill herself?" Okay, so yeah, maybe I had a freak out, but I was not okay with a diagnosis of bipolar disorder. I'm a completely normal girl. Well, at least I thought I was, and mental illness does not run in my family. So I should be exempt.

As I write to you today, I try and grasp portions of my past that may have flickered light into the possibility of a mental illness. In doing some research, I came across this journal entry from the end of my sophomore year of high school, one year before my first manic episode at Lake Powell.

Journal

July 14th, 2000

I can relate my life to a yin-yang. I am so involved in school and other activities that my day seems to fly by. I sometimes go from wonderful to the total opposite. I get so caught up in trying to help others solve their problems that I often forget about my own. Then it starts to build up, and I get so confused and stressed out.

My life is filled with so many things, and it plays with my emotions and feelings. I'm busy to the point that I literally burn out. This is the worst feeling. My week can vary day to day.

This is just like the yin-yang. Two different sides or feelings. I am one of those people who must talk about things on my mind in order to feel calm and secure again. I let little things go to my head and my imagination turns it into something it's not.

My personality can change somewhat easily. People really affect my mood and attitude. But in all honesty, it's me that changes, and I feel unbalanced. I don't know if I'm happy or sad, I just feel frustrated. And then the worry comes. I want and need to get rid of all my unnecessary worry, as it does nothing but waste time. Only I can control it. It's up to me.

I have to not only get over it, but do something about it. My life is very simple, but I make it so confusing. Is it that I feel better if I have something to worry about? Am I looking for something to bother me?

I worry about worrying. Tell me how crazy that sounds. I think I am at peace with myself, but it's like sometimes I'm afraid of my own thoughts. But why? It's my body, my mind, my thoughts and nobody controls them but me. So why not learn and understand every part of it, instead of letting my thoughts have a mind of their own?

I wish I could put some type of control on my thoughts. Then there wouldn't be so much uncertainty and I'd feel safer. I'd be calm.

My senior year of high school had begun, and I'd just been released from a psychiatric hospital in which I'd been tied down. I was still heavily medicated, and struggled gaining a sense of what had happened to me. The first few days of school were miserable, and I looked like I'd been run over by a truck. People talked. Girls stared. Teachers awkwardly smiled.

I did my best to hold it together and pretend as if nothing had happened. But then there were my eyes. I looked so drugged up, and my eyes dragged and drooped as if no life existed behind them. My soul was so incredibly tired.

I was the talk of the town, and my peers whispered behind my back. It was absolutely miserable and I can still feel the pain and sadness in the pit of my stomach as I write about it now. To be the center of someone's gossip is bad enough when you're a teenager, but in this situation...it felt like death. The depression that began felt like my soul was being crushed. The darkness was suffocating me.

So how could there be anything positive from this nightmare that was now my reality? I felt as if I would never feel the beauty of life again, and then it happened. I received a gift. I found her, or maybe we found each other, but she would be the biggest blessing of my life. She gave me purpose and ultimately helped me discover my real passion and purpose in this world. This gift is Dr. Elizabeth Caspian.

Prior to being released from the hospital in Phoenix, we were informed that I had to be released into the care of a psychiatrist. So back to the phone book my mom went. It was another moment of helplessness for my parents without solid support of how to handle my aftercare.

Now, I already had horrific experiences after several visits with Dr. Reed, the incredibly helpful Blue Rubber Band Lady. The doctors at the hospital were nothing short of traumatizing and paid no particular attention to me other than to pop pills down my throat.

So you can imagine I wasn't doing cartwheels to get back on the comfy couch with another wacko. But according to them, *I was the wacko*, so I guess I had to give it another shot. I'd fallen victim to stigma that said therapy is for crazy people. Those that are weak and helpless. I feared nothing more than being one of those people.

But then Dr. Caspian spoke to me. She spoke to me as a person and not as a patient. Even more so, she listened. I felt broken and ashamed, and she validated that it was okay for me to feel that way. We delighted in the fact that she could not only provide me with therapy, but also manage my medication.

This was decided indefinitely after Dr. Reed called Dr. Caspian when she found out I was seeing another doctor and yelled at her to "give her patient back." Dr. Reed insisted on getting her point across that Dr. Caspian was there simply to distribute medication and she needed to "back off." The phone call that my mom made to end services with Dr. Reed was…well, like a mama bear protecting her baby cub. I never saw Dr. Reed again.

Now, I realize that some people might say they like their psychiatrist because they give up the "good stuff" right? Well Dr. Caspian was just the opposite. The first thing she did when we began our work together was wean me off the massive amount of medication I was taking.

She told my parents that she couldn't believe I was even awake with the amount of medication the hospital had me on. In addition to my immensely supportive family, Dr. Caspian was my biggest advocate, and provided me the respect of being in the driver seat of my own healing.

I saw her nearly every other day for several months and each time I went, she really listened to me. She was fully present and engaged in every single session. I felt from her a sense of genuine interest and concern for my well being.

Literally an encyclopedia of knowledge, Dr. Caspian not only provided the therapy aspect of my recovery, but she allowed me to become an active part in the management of my medication. We talked about the brain, and the many ways it processes forms of trauma. I learned so much about what it really meant to be bipolar, and what was medically going on in my brain.

From her, I gained a true understanding that being bipolar is a chemical imbalance in your brain that affects your ability to regulate mood. I began to believe that it wasn't my fault and there was nothing I had done to cause this. Nor should I be ashamed of it.

I couldn't help that my brain lacked certain chemicals and produced more than needed of others. I was never handed a prescription without knowing exactly what it was, how it worked, what it would make me feel like, and what side effects may occur. Being the type of person that "needs all the details," I took great comfort in believing that I could ask her anything about my treatment and it would be treated with respect.

I valued that Dr. Caspian hoped to see me less regularly. Not because she didn't like working with me, but she wanted to help get me on my feet knowing that I was doing the hard work, and I didn't "need" her to get me through it.

The fewer times a week I saw her was viewed as a success. Not hers, but mine. She educated and empowered me to make my own decisions to improve my well being and mental health. Dr. Caspian also helped me deal with the difficulty of getting through my senior year with rumors flying and friends talking.

Over the years, I have had several of these friends apologize for not being there for me during the worst moments of my life. I valued their effort, but it came much too late and carried little effect. Although the hurt is now long gone, it sure was painful then.

Journal

October 22nd, 2001

Throughout all of this, I had this crazy thought in my head that I wanted to get out and about and spend time with my wonderful friends. Well, as it turns out, those friends aren't so wonderful. They don't call, they don't come by, they've done absolutely nothing. Now try and imagine here you are thinking about suicide, and the peers that are closest to you don't give a shit. As a seventeen year old, this is the most devastating news.

I've been so fucking mad at them because not a single one of them has been there for me when I needed it. Jenny has been supportive, and I'm thankful for that, but everyone else is too busy wrapped up in their own lives.

I would have given an arm and a leg for anyone of them, and it has been really difficult for me to forgive the fact that they haven't been there for me this year. I don't have the support I need, even after I shared what happened to me. I'm not sure if it's just that they don't understand, or they really don't care.

I was referring to the time I sat down two of my best friends and shared with them what I had been through. Even though they were on the trip at Lake Powell, they had only heard rumors about what had happened to me since.

It was two months into my senior year, and I felt that if I set the record straight, I would get my loving friends back. I knew that they weren't going to take the time to ask me, so I figured I'd cut them some slack and spill the beans.

I remember practicing with Dr. Caspian. She helped me find the courage and the words to finally set things straight and share what the last several months had been like for me. We rehearsed how I could share my experience in a way that didn't freak them out, but they would understand the severity of my condition. I was so insecure, and so fragile.

They had already been an absence in my life, but if there was a chance of salvaging any half ass relationship, I sure didn't want to ruin it. So I set a date. One day after school, I sat down with my two closest friends and told them everything. I explained what the mania felt like, how it was being in a mental hospital, the medication and daily visits to a psychiatrist. Feeling at least ten pounds lighter, I had done it. I had finally let down my wall enough to share my world of insanity with two other people.

I put my heart and soul out on the table, and as I let out a sigh of relief, the air that came back at me was stagnant and cold. They stared. They stared at me as if they were staring at a stranger. There were no supportive words, no sense of empathy, nor a hug in sight.

They followed up my rant with, "well let us know if you need anything," and left my house. *This has got to be a god damn joke.* I have known these girls for a majority of my life, and that was their response? I knew their words were empty, as they had never come through so far when I needed them.

I could have written my emotions and feelings on my forehead with a Sharpie marker and they wouldn't have even blinked. As time went by, my fury and hatred for people continued. The depression thickened as I felt like I lived under a dark cloud that wouldn't stop raining on me. Everyone else had umbrellas.

Journal

April 3rd, 2002

My thoughts seem so crazy and emotional. This is all too familiar. I feel so angry. I am not mad at my parents, but I'm sure it seems like I am. I just wish I had the love and support from my friends that I have from my family.

I have been trying so hard to move on and forgive them for not being there for me, but I don't think I can do it. Why should I have to? Friends are supposed to be there in times of need. Obviously I'm hanging out with the wrong group of friends, and have been since I was little. I just wish that other people knew what I was going through. I have a problem asking for help, so I show them with my body, either losing or gaining weight.

Sometimes I cut myself. When the bleeding leaves a trail of my secret outlet for pain, I'll burn myself instead. I'll put an empty pot on the stove and wait for it to heat up, and then I'll hold my arm or hands on it as long as I can until I pull back in pain.

It sounds fucking crazy, but it always feels good once the pain lessens. I feel so angry, and the easiest person to take it out on is myself.

My senior year was almost over and the University of Arizona waited for me just around the corner. Much of my senior year was a blur. Drowsy eyes and lack of interest followed me everywhere.

Friends were few and far between. Actually, let me rephrase that. I had a ton of friends and continued my time in the popular circle. I was the captain of the Varsity Cheerleading squad, a member of the Student Council, nominated for Homecoming and Prom Queen and made a 3.8 GPA. It was one of the most miserable and lonely years I can remember.

While I was surrounded by people, the friends that really mattered to me spent their time putting powder up their noses. I couldn't interrupt their party driven lives with any of my miniscule problems. The effort it took to paste a smile on my face to hide the devastation I felt was immense. It left me with nothing else to give at the end of the day.

While friends gathered for lunch off campus every day, I drove home and sobbed in my room alone. This was the only way I could keep it together enough to make it through the afternoon. Clean yourself up Erin, fix your makeup...5th hour starts in 15 minutes.

It was May 16th, 2002 and a day I'll never forget. I walked through the doors of my high school in my typically late fashion. Ms. Berry wouldn't have known what to do if I showed up on time. I entered the classroom and as I walked to my desk, I got "the look." It had been awhile since I'd gotten the look. This time was different though, as it wasn't the judgmental stare, it was the "she definitely didn't get the memo" stare.

I dropped my backpack close by my desk and slid into my seat. Derek sat in front of me, and we had been friends since Kindergarten. He turned around in his seat and asked if I was okay. I hesitantly said "yes," with a drawn out pause and asked, "Why?" He replied, "You didn't hear?"

As my heart sank into my stomach, the next line was one of the most gut wrenching sentences to come out of one's mouth. "Marie killed herself," he whispered. With a sense of horror and disbelief, I stood up and ran from the room not knowing if I was going to vomit. Tears poured from my eyes like I'd been storing them up for years.

I walked toward the common area of the school where the crew would hang out, called the "blue blocks." There, I found a group of my friends who obviously already knew. For the first time in a long time, I was comforted.

We sat together hugging and crying for what seemed like forever. Our school counselor, the mother of another one of my very good childhood friends, approached me on the blue blocks. She asked me to come into her office, and I did.

At this point the school had not received confirmation that it was Marie that passed away. But they received a report from the Sheriff's office that two days earlier, on May 14th, a girl that graduated from my high school the previous year had committed suicide. Her name was Marie, but no last name was confirmed. I had to make the call.

I picked up the phone to dial Marie's best friend in the world, Leah, a very close friend of mine as well. I asked if she had heard the same news I'd just received. The fact that Leah was absent from school that day already confirmed my fears. She was crying, we both were.

I could hear the anger in her voice. The school counselor called my mom and she rushed from work to be with me. In a circle of friends and family, we left school together and I felt fortunate to have the love and support I did at that moment.

We stuck together for Marie. She needed us to find comfort and healing so that she could rest peacefully. Days passed and the memorial service was held. The church was packed with broken hearted teenagers and devastated family members. I prayed that Marie could see how much we all loved her.

Dr. Caspian was crucial in helping me grieve the loss of a close friend. Although I was impatient, she knew it would take time, just as it had taken time for me to heal from the traumatic effects of my own journey. Experiencing the loss of close friend helped put my life into perspective. I share this story, because I know how prevalent suicide is among teens and young adults. Especially those who suffer from a mental illness.

Although I may or may not have been able to help her, I gained insight into how important it is for young people to have conversations about the reality of their feelings, and create a social network that is open and supportive.

I was so thankful to have Dr. Caspian in my life. We spent many sessions talking about Marie over the next month, and I was able to grieve her loss and grow from the privilege I had of knowing her.

As I moved forward in my own healing, I brought the focus back to preparing for the year of college just months away. It was my last summer in Flagstaff and I needed to stay focused on the future so I could flee from that horrible place.

Dr. Caspian and I spent time discussing that word. Bipolar. Both she and I had doubts that bipolar disorder was my true diagnosis; therefore she gave me no diagnosis. My chart read, MD-NOS (mood disorder not otherwise specified).

I appreciated the fact that she wasn't quick to slap me with a label. There was no doubt that whatever happened to me earlier that year was some kind of mental break. But I was struggling with the fact that I had been taking medications to treat bipolar disorder all year, and I wasn't really sure if I was bipolar.

My meds kept me somewhat neutral, and I didn't have any major spurts of "crazy" throughout the year. But I didn't want to take medication for the rest of my life if I didn't need to. So Dr. Caspian let me decide.

She said that if I did in fact suffer from bipolar disorder and I went off my medication, I would most likely have another episode. We didn't know when that episode would occur, but it was somewhat inevitable. I figured it was time to find out, so the summer after my senior year of high school, I slowly went off all my medication.

While my doctor and family didn't think it was the right time to go about changing or going off my meds, I was 18. And you know how well 18 year olds listen to their parents. So they supported me in doing it in the safest way possible, with a great deal of supervision.

My parents and brother were there for me every step of the way. August of 2002 had come and I was almost completely off all of my meds. I had packed up for college, and things were moving along just fine.

7 HI MANIA, IT'S ME AGAIN

My brother Adam was a junior at the University of Arizona in Tucson and was just as excited for me to come to college as I was. He was in the Delta Chi fraternity and had a group of friends that had already been in my life for the last two years. They were like my older brothers and I took comfort in the fact that I already knew some people. They knew my history.

Typically I didn't want anyone to know, but they did and I appreciated that. I felt like if anything were to happen to me, I would be taken care of. And I was. Thank God for Adam, because within eight days of leaving for college, I was back in the hospital. Now I know what you're thinking, and yes, I flew off the deep end! Shit, not again!

It was rush week. Greek life at U of A is an enormous part of college. I was so excited to rush a sorority, and find a new group of friends that really appreciated who I was. Young people covered the campus and filled the dorms, which created a whole new sense of freedom and opportunity for me.

The first week of college life started out amazing. There were new faces that invited you into their circle of friends and filled your cup with beer at the same time. It was everything an eighteen year old girl could possibly want after driving out of a town that had formerly been her nightmare.

As I've now come to realize, my inability to sleep, night after night, is a major red flag for an oncoming episode. But with all of the fun I was having, and meeting girls in my dorm, there was so much to do, and so little time. I felt incredible.

I felt euphoric in a way that people who have interactions with God himself feel. I finally had energy that never seemed to cease. I felt happiness so deep down in my soul that it made my body tingle. Day by day, I slept less and less, and I began losing sense of reality. Again.

Now, you might say, "Well, if you know you aren't sleeping and you can feel yourself getting manic, why don't you just take a sleeping pill and shut your mind off?" Unfortunately, it doesn't work that way. I didn't realize how bad it was becoming until I was completely out of control. It's like trying to explain to a drunken person that they've had too much to drink.

In their mind, everything is fine. They feel good, really good, and nothing you tell them is going to make sense in the reality that they currently live in. I was becoming so distracted and removed from reality; I struggled remembering to complete daily tasks.

Like... go to class...pick up groceries...drink water... buy notebooks. The girls in my dorm room hall could see how "all over the place" I was becoming, so they started leaving me post it notes all around my room to help keep me focused.

Once the delirium had really taken flight, I went over to my brother's fraternity and spoke to him in a way that made him realize the seriousness of my condition. I told him something that held stagnant in the air and dripped with concern. "I've been talking to Marie, and she's doing wonderful up there. I've got it all figured out."

Talking to the deceased had not previously been a gift of mine, and the fact that I'd suddenly discovered it and was dying to tell Adam about her in the afterlife was frightening to say the least. My parents took the call from my brother, and they knew. I was off my meds, and this was the episode we had crossed our fingers wouldn't come.

A series of events took place in the time it took my parents to make the four hour drive to Tucson. After walking into oncoming traffic, I remember lying down on the concrete sidewalk in the middle of campus, as strangers walked cautiously around me. I liked the way the clouds moved, and I felt the ability to control their speed.

I was nearly arrested in my college dorm, when I went stomping into another girl's room and began trashing it. The bowl of cereal being held in front of her was splashed away as my hand smacked the bowl from underneath.

This girl was completely random, I had never met her, but I wildly threw things around the room as if we were in a violent fight. I had no clue what I was doing. All sense of appropriateness was lost.

Fortunately, my brother Adam happened to call my cell phone during this time, and the Resident Assistant from that hall answered. She informed my brother that I was out of control and the police were going to be called.

He begged them frantically not to call the police, and explained that I had a medical condition. They agreed that if the RA could keep me calm, and my brother came over immediately to pick me up, the police would not be called. He assured them that he lived just across campus and would be there in a matter of minutes.

Once Adam arrived at my dorm, I sat curled up on the floor, holding my knees to my chest, crying. I didn't understand what was happening but I knew that people were angry with me. I was spewing out words at rapid speed, talking about heaven, and I grew more frustrated about the confusion I couldn't get rid of.

My parents drove to Tucson and they officially knew. It had finally happened, and I was having another episode. They drove me back to my dorm room to gather some of my belongings and think through their next steps. It was clear that my stay at U of A had come to a halt.

As I gathered my things, it dawned on me that they were taking me away from college, which I was not pleased about. I became very angry and began screaming at them for ruining my life. I refused to leave the dormitory lobby and get in the car. There was no way I was leaving this bliss, and especially not with *those* people. The people who didn't understand that I had things all figured out.

With my mom and dad on each side of me, they lifted me up by my arms and feet and carried me into the car. I was kicking and screaming bloody murder for them to release me. The watching eyes must have thought I was being abducted. I ended up with a scratch on my side which I later convinced myself was all a ploy for my abusive parents to hold me against my will.

My poor mom and dad had no other choice. They were horrified and unbelievably concerned about me. Watching me struggle truly broke their hearts. All of my life, my mom and dad have been my very best friends. But now…they were lost and swimming upstream against a vicious current. They had no idea what to do next, yet held on to every ounce of strength they had so they could remain strong for me.

My parents drove me to a hotel on the west side of campus, where we would stay for a few hours so they could gather their thoughts and make a game plan. We pulled up parallel to the hotel curb and both of my parents car doors opened.

My anger for them was still in full effect, and I refused to get out of the car. I insisted that I needed to be sent with the car through the valet line. Rules didn't apply to me. They could find me in the parking lot if they needed me, curled up in a ball in the back seat of their Chevy Tahoe.

At this point, my parents had spoken to Dr. Caspian nearly a million times. She was helping to guide their next steps. My parents were walking on eggshells, with every few minute being different than the last. Like coaxing a small child to take a nap, my parents convinced me to get out of the car and go up to the hotel room with them. Once I stepped out of the car, my mood changed and went off to a much kinder place.

I was suddenly euphoric and grandiose. The breeze felt amazing, and the sun shined brighter. When the wind touched my face, it peaked the interest of every hair follicle on my face and danced with it playfully. I was on a high I never wanted to leave and I cherished the dream-like realm I was currently in. I loved the way my body felt, it was more alive than I'd ever known possible.

While in the hotel room, I did a number of humiliating things. I started with my dad's suitcase. I emptied all of his clothing out on the bed and item by item, I refolded it. Then I moved on to his toiletry kit and lined up all the contents along the top of the dresser.

The cologne, deodorant, eye drops, vitamins, etc. They had to be in perfect order, lined up from shortest to tallest. The items stood taller and straighter for me than they had for anyone else.

Next, I found the most brilliant tube of red lipstick in my mom's purse. I began smearing it around my mouth, above and below my lips, nearing my nose and chin. I looked like a circus reject with no filter for what was socially appropriate.

I laughed with delight at my new found confidence and freedom. I remember my parents putting me in bed to keep me from roaming around. They tucked the covers in tight around me and hoped that if only I could fall asleep, it might keep the mania from continuing down the path to a full blown episode.

But then it happened again. I wet the bed. Multiple times. Covered in lipstick and urine, my mom helped me out of bed and walked me toward the bathroom to bathe. I didn't wait until I got there.

Instead, I immediately stripped off my shirt and bra and stood topless in front of my dad. He dropped his head in sheer embarrassment and confusion about what had happened to his little girl. My dad knew that when I "came to," this act would be absolutely humiliating for me. Just as it was for him.

My mom led me to the bathroom where I took off the rest of my clothing and got into the warm bathtub. I leaned back and spread my arms out and legs open as the euphoria of the warm water came over me. Again, all discretion went out the window, and wearing the humiliation on her face for me, my mom began to bathe me.

This episode seemed to have much more meaning than the first. After my sponge bath, I began filling out the hotel feedback cards as if they were cards to God. I wanted to be sure to tell Him all of the pleasures I was experiencing, and how much I appreciated my conversations with Marie.

Words all seemed to connect. Every song on the radio had a hidden meaning, and was written only for me. I knew the words of songs I had never heard before. Street signs were all significant and carried personal messages that I could capture without explanation.

I remember taking a yellow highlighter to a TIME magazine and as I flipped through, I highlighted all the different words that spoke to my soul. Names of people in my life, places I'd been, and phrases that carried significant meaning. I felt a deep sense of connection in the world, and had suddenly inherited wisdom unknown to any other human being.

As if Jesus had chosen me to spread the message of His word, and the serendipity of life, I was important. I wanted to do everything in my power to fulfill this heaven sent duty. I found comfort and purpose; I was on top of the world.

With much effort and frustration that evening, my parents packed up our stuff from the hotel in Tucson, and we got back on the road for the four hour drive to Flagstaff. It was a nightmare of a trip for them. Just the beginning of a series of nightmarish moments with me.

A couple of hours had gone by, and we ended up pulling off to some flea bag motel in the middle of nowhere so my parents could try and get a few hours of sleep. I spent the next 3 hours turning on and off the lights in the room, and biting my nails off as I sat on the bathroom floor when my parents hushed me and told me to sit still.

With dark, tired eyes, my parents got out of bed once again, put me back in the car, and we drove the rest of the way home. I was so difficult to be around. I acted like a three year old that got into everything and had no concern for my own safety. I lacked all common sense and had zero interest in anything beyond the words, sounds and feelings related to my own importance.

We made it back to Flagstaff, and Dr. Caspian instructed my parents not to leave my side, as I needed 24/7 supervision. My mom went to the bathroom with me, my dad followed me into the kitchen and they both slept downstairs on couches close to my bedroom each night.

The summer before I left for U of A, I began dating Joey. When I withdrew from school and returned home with my parents, he was right there by my side. I had known him since I was a little girl, so our relationship moved fairly quickly. He was so supportive and my parents had kept him in the loop of everything that had been happening at U of A. Joey traded shifts with my parents and he watched me as I wandered around the house. It was only when I was with him would I sleep.

Joey was the only one that I didn't fight with when I had to take the medication I'd gotten back on. He would hold it out for me in his palm as if I were a child. My parents knew he was the best thing for me at the time, so he slept with me each night and watched as I twitched and rambled in my dreams. My parents were so thankful to have him there, and so was I.

Spending time with me was everything but pleasant. My parents lived in constant worry and concern, and I lived in constant anger and irritation. I didn't understand why they couldn't just leave me the hell alone. I was an eighteen year old woman!

Finally my rage had built up enough and I broke out in a fury against them. After they refused to let me sit outside the house on the curb all night, I walked back inside to my bedroom as they followed along behind me. Standing there battling them to leave me alone, I screamed in their faces, "I fucking hate you!"

Although they knew I was ill at the time, it has always been something I wish I could have taken back. They were doing everything in their power to keep me safe, and I can only imagine how heart wrenching this experience was for them.

I feel sadness deep inside even as I think of it now. They were the two most incredible people in my life, showing me continuous love and support. Yet, I wanted nothing they had to offer. I wanted to be alone.

Completely exhausted and drained of energy, my parents were instructed by Dr. Caspian to hospitalize me again. Simply put, they could not follow me around each and every day. They had not slept for days on end, and were consumed with sadness and fear for what I would do next. At that point, hospitalization was the level of care I needed.

My mom packed me a duffle bag of clothes and toiletries and told me we were on our way to meet with Dr. Caspian at her new office. I was thrilled! I hadn't seen her since I'd left for college! I had been working so closely with her all year, and I could not wait to share my new found sense of connection to life.

The "new office" they spoke of was the behavioral health unit at our local hospital. At this point, I was 18, so my parents could not check me in, I had to consent. With some loving manipulation, I signed all the papers and my parents had to leave their daughter behind those heavy locked doors…again.

There they stood on the other side of the double pane glass looking in at their daughter they had lost once more. Their souls were shattered and they had so many unanswered questions.

All the while, they were expected to go about their day, show up to work and put on the fake smile that was barely able to cover up the pain. They did what they needed to at work, while holding back the tears that their daughter was having another mental breakdown.

During this go-round at the hospital, I was in the adult unit in Flagstaff, which was beneficial as there was a greater focus on support groups and self reflection. Overdosing me on antipsychotics was also not a part of the plan, so that was a step in the right direction.

However, it was terrifying. I remember a Native American man that stayed a few doors down from me. His hair draped down his back to the top of his pants, and his eyes were dark and empty. He would wander the halls at all hours of the night, wearing nothing but a hospital gown and socks.

He paced up and down the hall, back and forth and then stopped in front of my room and stared for minutes at a time. No words were ever spoken, but the precarious look on his face made me afraid of what he might do or say. He did that periodically throughout each and every day.

My room was similar to the one in the first hospital, except that I was on the first floor and had a large window that looked upon the parking lot outside. Two beds stood on either side of the window, mine against the wall on the right. Underneath the window was a night stand for myself and my roommate.

My roommate was a real hoot. She was probably seventy five years old and carried around an oxygen tank with her, which always kept me up at night. The sounds of her mechanically assisted breathing combined with her constant passing gas created a cacophony like a musical in our shared room.

She wore glasses that fell crooked on her face, and I eventually realized this was due to a missing arm from the frame meant to rest upon her ear. So of course they were lopsided!

But her creativity set in, and she took a piece of Scotch tape and placed it vertically over the bridge of her nose between her eyebrows to hold the glasses in place. It was insanely (pardon the pun) strange looking, but quite clever if you ask me.

I remember another man who was detoxing from methamphetamine and alcohol. He almost died while I was there. Each trip to the emergency room left the group wondering if he would ever come back. Shivering and sweating, he would sit on the couch wearing his blue New York Yankees hat and tell me, "Listen darling, don't you ever take the road I've taken. You've got too much life ahead of you."

The adults in the hospital seemed to take care of me, as many of them had children my age. Not the most wonderful experience of my life, but I took with me some valuable lessons. Each day we sat together in group and explored our emotions, feelings and coping mechanisms.

I was actually able to start participating during my visit there. Despite telling other patients, "I don't know why I'm here," I soon realized that I was actually sick.

There were several other people there with a bipolar diagnosis, which was a combination of comforting and horrifying. I had never been around anyone else that had similar experiences to mine, and that gave me a sense of normalcy. Yet the fact that they were 30 years older than me and still going through bouts of suicide attempts, mania and drug use frightened me. I didn't want to feel like this forever.

I sat outside chain smoking cigarettes with the group of my newly found friends. There is such a sense of bonding when you smoke, especially when you combine smokers who are mentally ill and addicted to drugs.

Holy lord, did we have some good conversations. Nothing was off limits. Some people would "one up" another person's story by sharing how much crazier they were, so "listen to this."

We spoke of experiences of pain and hope, which in turn brought the group close and we reminded each other why living was a good idea. One woman, Anna pointed to the 6 inch scar across her throat and said, "Don't give up," after sharing with us that she had taken a switchblade to her neck a few years back.

8 WHEN FOOD BECOMES MY LIFE

I stayed at the hospital in Flagstaff for 5 days, and during that time they put me on a 10 mg dose of Zyprexa, which helped stabilize me. I remained withdrawn from U of A that semester and took a few classes at the local Community College.

I felt like such a loser. A lunatic, drop out, living at home with her parents. Awesome. How did my life seriously come to this? I really screwed up somewhere along the line, because I am pathetic.

The only beauty of it was that I continued dating Joey, who had come with my parents every day to see me in the hospital. On my windowsill was the Styrofoam cup he took a pen to and scribbled flowers and funny pictures on to remind me that it was okay to laugh again.

It was wonderful to have someone helping me in addition to my parents. I could trust him with anything, and he had seen me in the worst of situations. He hadn't run for the hills, so I knew I had his love and approval. I felt so safe with Joey.

My family was utterly grateful for all that he did for me; he was like a son to them. I would end up spending the next 5 years, off and on with him. But it wasn't easy. Sure, he had his own struggles, but being bipolar was such a burden to me. It took time and much frustration for me to manage my moods and crawl through the darkness of depression.

That semester in Flagstaff was incredibly tough. I cried all the time. Sleeping was the only thing I wanted to do, and I needed the room dark and closed off. Leave me there and I'll come out when I'm ready. If ever. I preferred to get at least 12 hours of sleep a night and got incredibly irritated when my parents made me get out from under the covers.

I had no interest in seeing people or doing anything I liked. I didn't even know what I liked anymore. I'd lost who I was. My identity was gone and I felt like I had nothing to build from. I couldn't remember the fun Erin. Depression is one of the most suffocating experiences I have ever felt.

This state of being is far beyond the emotional understanding of feeling sad. It's much deeper than that. Sadness is just the tip of the iceberg and only scratches the surface of the true nature of throbbing pain. It's the G rated version of pain. We all experience sadness. We don't all experience the depression that makes us idolize the thought of death.

It felt like the loss of a soul, encapsulated in the weight of the world. It's an absolute disconnect from believing that one's purpose in this life is important. That purpose even exists. It's the suicide of a mental state that keeps someone from being able to seek truth, solace and comfort in the world we live in.

The current space they take up in this world does not hold them in a way that allows them to view their pain as temporary. The memories of feeling happiness and ease were out of my reach. That was foreign to me now.

I spent most of my time at home with my parents, Jenny and Joey. Hidden away from the rumors that flew around town just as they did one year prior.

I was weak and hated myself for not being able to go off to college and prove to people that I was normal again. I had failed and I was such a fool because of it. I was so insecure. I had gained 20 pounds on the medication I was taking, and I felt like a rhino pumped up with crazy pills.

I felt disgusting and battled with the idea of having to take medication forever. I could stop taking it, and lose the weight, but we all knew how that would end up. Instead, I was a fat pile of crap and dependant on pills.

I knew that I needed the medication to get healthy, but I was equally sickened by that fact. I was supposed to fight this battle on my own. I was supposed to show people how strong I was. Struggling through my moods and managing my depression began to greatly affect my relationship with Joey, my parents and my friends.

Journal

October 20th, 2002

I am so self conscious about my body. Everything looks different to me, even my face looks fat. I feel tired, sad, overweight, irritable and angry. There are so many things that I want to go out and do, but I just feel so lonely.

I want to get better so I can show people that I don't need them to care for me. But when I wake up and feel like this, I know I need help. I don't think I can get out of bed today. I have no idea what makes me happy anymore. I have felt so tired and lazy since taking Zyprexa and its making me gain weight.

My irritability has been so bad lately, so Dr. Caspian increased my meds to Wellbutrin twice a day and more Zyprexa at night. She thinks that it might be a side effect of the Wellbutrin, or I might not be taking a high enough dosage.

It's been a few months since I left college, and I feel miserable. I feel so fat, and I feel like food is ruining me. I've been so depressed with this whole bipolar thing and I've been eating a lot lately. Dr. Caspian and I have considered taking Lithium, since Zyprexa causes significant weight gain. But I have heard nothing but bad things about Lithium, so that really scares me.

Another thing on my mind is Marie. Her birthday was on the 14th and it's been five months since she died. I know that I will think about her throughout my life, but I just miss her so much.

This is so hard. I wish I could talk to her, because she would understand like nobody else has. I knew she was taking Depakote, and she could identify with how it feels. She's been through some of these problems, and I regret not openly talking about bipolar disorder before.

I feel like I could have helped her, and she could have helped me. At least someone would know what it feels like.

The first semester of my freshman year in Flagstaff came to a close, and while I made good grades at the Community College, I still felt worthless. I struggled from August to December with the heaviness of serious depression, and spent week by week with Dr. Caspian trying to work on my image and self esteem.

I was not at all comfortable with having a mental illness, nor did I want anyone knowing that I was different. I was damaged. I spent so much time hiding behind a mask so that people in my town didn't think I wasn't strong enough to fight this. I feared showing vulnerability more than I feared death.

I was ready to get back to U of A in Tucson, and put all of this behind me. Go back to a place where nobody knew that I was crazy. Where nobody knew I didn't usually weigh this much, and somewhere that I could make up who I wanted to be without them knowing the truth. Yet there was a part of me that felt so nervous.

What if it happens again? What if my meds stop working? What if I can't ever get out of bed? What if no one likes me? But I had to push those thoughts aside and connect with the deeply hidden confident Erin that knew she had lots to offer the world.

I moved back to Tucson in January of 2003 and lived in a different dorm (thank God, I was so embarrassed about the last incident of almost being arrested). I lived with another girl, who was really sweet and we got along, but we didn't share much of a connection to develop a long term friendship.

Starting school in the middle of the year was much harder than I had expected. I found that many people had already found their circle of friends and were settled into a routine. I also continued to gain weight, which added to my insecurity. I felt especially insecure because it seemed as if most of the girls at U of A paired their size two frame with amazing legs and fake boobs. Shit.

Journal

January 21ˢᵗ, 2003

I have a problem. I don't know if I'm bulimic or what, but for the past three or four months, I make myself throw up after I eat. I completely binge and eat everything in sight so that I can throw it back up. I didn't write about this before now, because I've been afraid to actually get it down on paper.

But months have gone by now and I can't stop making myself throw up. I like to eat, but then once I do, I feel so guilty and can't relax until I throw it up. It's not like its even making me lose weight.

I'm scared because food completely controls my life. It's all I can ever think of. I wish I could be normal and not worry about it, but once I think about it, I have to binge and throw up. NOBODY knows about this. I really want to stop, but I've tried and I can't. I usually vomit three or four times a day.

So many things are going through my mind. I'm back here in Tucson again, but it's so much different than I thought it would be. This has been a huge adjustment, one that I wasn't really ready for.

This first month of school I've spent crying to my parents, Jenny and Joey. I feel so alone and completely overwhelmed. Things vary for me from day to day, and sometimes I miss all of my classes.

I now know that I suffered from Bulimia; however I was too afraid to put such a label on it at the time. It was my secret, and the one thing I felt I had control of in my life. It was mine and I owned it. But it didn't take long for it to have full control of me.

I remember feeling frantic. I would stuff my face with ice cream, yogurt, pasta, or pizza. Anything that comes up easily was really tempting for me. When I binged, I would feel panicked and out of control. It was almost a euphoric high. I ate quickly as if it was my last meal, and my world was spiraling downward.

Once I realized how much I had eaten, I would freak out because I knew how much fatter it would make me. I couldn't handle another pound. Then once I threw up, I felt an overwhelming sense of relief. But the relief was short lived, because then guilt would take over my mind.

I knew what I was doing was unhealthy, but it seemed to have such power over me. About 7 months in to my bulimia, I told my parents. They were shocked, but completely supportive. At this point there was nothing that I couldn't tell them and nothing they wouldn't help get me through.

 I also reached out to Dr. Caspian and let her know that my eating habits were completely taking over my life. I was so afraid that she would be disappointed in me. I had fallen down again, but in a different arena of life. How embarrassing.

I would plan my day based around when I could eat and where I could purge. I was afraid to eat in front of people, because of the maniacal way I shoveled in the food, knowing that minutes later, it would come back up. I also had to plan when I could make my escape from the table because I had to go alone. The bathroom would have to be empty for me to follow through on my secretive plan.

I'd map out my "barfing spots" throughout campus. Some bathrooms were less crowded at certain times of the day, and other bathrooms played music in the background, which would drown out my gags. Not only was this binge-purge game damaging me emotionally, but I was not getting the nutrition I needed, nor was I keeping down my medication. Dr. Caspian and I spoke about seeking support from an eating disorder specialist.

Journal

February 3rd, 2003

I've been having a really bad day. I had apple juice and a fruit shake for breakfast but then I had to go to lunch with someone, which always freaks me out. I ate some baked ziti and a breadstick and I immediately came home and threw up. That was around 3:00pm. It's now 8:30pm and I'm still binging.

I hate this shit so much. It's like a rush to binge and I'm happy while I'm doing it. But once it's over, I feel fat and panicked, so the only way to feel better is to throw up.

Why do I have to do this all the time? All I can ever think of is what I am gonna eat, how much, and when and where I can throw it up. I've been too tired from throwing up to work out today.

I hate my body so much it hurts. Sometimes once I'm done throwing up, I just get in the shower and cry. I feel so sad and ashamed. I hate myself so much sometimes, and just wish I had a body to be proud of. I weigh 180 pounds and it's disgusting. Yeah, I'm 5'10, but I would die if anyone knew I weighed that much. I want to lose weight so bad, but I'm in this terrible cycle of binging and purging and don't know how to get out.

After about 2 years, I did overcome my bulimia. I worked with an eating disorder specialist and tracked my eating habits. I had to document every time I binged and purged, I ranked my daily mood, what time I took my medication and how much sleep I got each night.

That journal helped me recognize how much the bulimia was affecting my mood and the management of my medication. My health was also deteriorating. I had no metabolism, my gums began to peel, I ended up with 5 cavities, and my nails stopped growing. The specialist recommended vitamins, which seemed to help get my strength back.

I returned to Flagstaff in May of 2003 for summer break and spent that time with Joey and other friends. It was one of the most amazing summers I could remember. Things had started to get much better, my meds were doing their job and I felt more stable than I had in years. Plus, I was sleeping every night. Score!

Finally, after 2 years of hell, my life seemed to get back on track, and it hasn't majorly derailed from those train tracks since. Trust me, I have my downfalls, my panic moments, and my sad days, but they are nowhere near as detrimental as before. My coping skills have much improved.

My parents advocated on my behalf when I returned to U of A and enrolled me with the Disability Resource Center so that I could have special accommodations made for me.

I often needed to miss class if I went nights without sleep, was going through medication changes, or required more time to finish tests. Finals were especially difficult for me, because I wasn't that average college student that could *pull an all nighter*. That was the recipe for disaster.

I continued to have therapy sessions with Dr. Caspian via phone regularly and also drove to Flagstaff for in person visits. My parents also went to Dr. Caspian so they could learn how to help me maintain my health and stability, and also get the support that they needed to heal.

The experience that they went through was no less tragic than my own experience of going through it. My parents needed and deserved help to process the trauma they had been through as well.

We were a team determined to make it to the finish line. My mom and dad were my biggest cheerleaders and we spoke on the phone daily as they helped me find "Erin" again.

They normalized my experiences and did their best to remove my sense of guilt, blame and embarrassment. I don't know that I would have gotten to the place of peace and acceptance as I have now without their guidance. My parents helped show me that my disorder didn't define me.

So there it is. Now the world knows my story. All of my dirty laundry, out there in the open...I'm vulnerable, weak and exposed. I'm also free, and IT FEELS SO GOOD! I have written about some of the deepest, darkest and most painful experiences of my life within these pages.

Why? I'm speaking out, openly and honestly about my experience with bipolar disorder with the hope that it might make a difference.

This book was placed in your hands for a reason, and I deeply hope that it serves as an inspiration for overcoming the many obstacles that come along with a mental illness.

9 PUTTING THE PIECES BACK TOGETHER

Over a decade later, I still remember how the word bipolar disorder clothed me with disgust unlike any embarrassment or shame I'd ever felt. It suffocated me and along with it came terror as my mind replayed media stories that captured the lunatics that also shared this horrific label.

For years I felt as though the word itself was the new defining factor of who I was as a person. It was my purpose, my limited value, and my narrowing, tragic future. Bipolar was my identity similar to my curly hair and freckled face. It remained there...but not forever.

Around the age of 20, I accepted the fact that bipolar disorder had already purchased property in my mind. It had moved in the boxes, and claimed it as its own.

Bipolar disorder didn't check in with me to see if the space was available for rent, and there was no cost negotiation. There was no going back. The purchase was made with an expiration date of forever, no signature necessary.

After all these years of being "in the ring" with bipolar disorder, I am the one calling the shots. Could this mood disorder make a swift uppercut and get a quick jab in while I'm focusing my attention on living life?

Sure, but the likelihood of that jab drawing blood or knocking me to the ground is slim. I've spent too much time training, my protective gear is top of the line, and my reflexes are ten times faster than what they use to be.

After two hospitalizations, debilitating depression, dropping out of college, and battling an eating disorder, I made a choice. I learned new coping skills. I wasn't willing to tap out.

While I couldn't change the fact that I had bipolar disorder, I could take charge of the impact in which it affected my life. I wanted to parade around inside of that ring, a champion, with my arms held high and my chest pumping with pride. I craved an authentic applause, one that I knew I was worthy of. I was no longer willing to let bipolar disorder bully me around.

This is when I had to "buy in." I bought into the fact that I am living with a mental illness. It is necessary for me to take medication to manage this illness, and I feel fortunate to be living with a disorder that is treatable.

Once I bought into the idea that bipolar disorder and I were lifetime roommates sharing the same cereal and closet space, my life completely changed. Here are a few things I learned:

1. Feeling better means that my medication is working, therefore I must keep taking it.

2. Quit worrying about what other people think or say
    about me. My time is much too valuable.

3. I am still completely capable of success. Nothing is
    out of my reach.

4. I will have to work on my health and wellbeing
    regularly. Self care is a lifestyle, not an option.

5. Therapy and I will never breakup. It is the sustenance
    to my healing.

6. I must create a support system that doesn't have
    limitations or ultimatums.

7. I refuse to feel ashamed of something I can't control.
    It's a wasted emotion.

8. There is purpose and meaning in my struggle.

9. I have the ability to define myself.

10. Nobody is living this life but me. I'm going to make
    it count.

So how did I get from there to here? Let me fast
forward and get you up to date. When I went started my
sophomore year at U of A, I joined Alpha Phi Sorority, where
I established friendships with some of the most amazing
women.

The four years I spent at U of A were nothing short of amazing. It was the college experience I'd always wanted. I surrounded myself with people who were genuine and we took care of each other as if we were family. Did I deal with ups and downs? Absolutely.

I still had bouts of depression, I self harmed from time to time when I felt overwhelmed, and experienced several panic attacks. But I had built a solid support system, and was able to get out of the darkness much quicker than I had in the past. I knew the red flags of when I was starting to go sideways.

In May 2007, I graduated from college with a degree in Elementary Education and moved back to Flagstaff. I was thrilled to be home, and my town no longer carried the feeling of disgust and hatred like I'd once felt about it.

My off and on relationship with Joey over the last 5 years came to an end a few months after I moved home. We tried living together and realized it was time for both of us to move forward and take the next step in our lives as individuals.

Shortly after that, I got a job. And hold onto your knickers, because you won't believe who I worked for! Dr. Caspian! She offered me a job to be her assistant where I answered phones, organized charts and set dates for appointments.

It was not necessarily my dream job, but I had an incredible amount of respect for Dr. Caspian and the opportunity to work for and learn from her was such an honor. She had been my mentor for the last 5 years.

About a year later, I began working as an advocate at a domestic violence shelter for women and children, where I became the Shelter Manager for the next three years. It was one of the most amazing opportunities I've had in my entire life.

I learned about the experiences of other women and the traumas they had endured. They were such survivors and although the stories they told were horrific, the strength they carried absolutely changed my life. They inspired me.

They spoke of being manipulated, coerced, beaten, tortured, threatened, and sexually abused. They survived things no person should ever have to go through. And so did their children. But they were still standing, and hanging on to every fiber of hope they had.

These women didn't give up, not like I wanted to. When I felt all alone, I wanted to die. When they felt all alone, they were glad to still be alive. I learned about how damaged the human soul can be, but also how strong our souls become when we open our hearts and minds to healing. These are what I like to call Soul Moments.

These are moments when something in your life happens and your soul is changed for the better. You grow and take on a better version of yourself. I pray that each and every one of us is sometime touched with Soul Moments.

In the midst of my highs and lows I have accomplished a lot. I am now 29 and have experienced a multitude of beautiful opportunities. During my 3 years at the domestic violence shelter, I worked with women from all walks of life. Many of them were also diagnosed with bipolar disorder.

I played the advocate role, set healthy professional boundaries and did not disclose any of my personal experiences. Not because I didn't want to, but I always wanted to ensure that my work with them was about their healing, not mine. Being a part of how other people experience mental illness gave me so much strength.

My mental illness has allowed me the empathy and compassion to work with other people experiencing mental illness. I know what it's like. It hit so close to home, and I prayed that the women I was helping would receive some of the blessings that I had. Unlike many, I had beautiful parents that walked through every painful step with me. Not everyone has the privilege of that type of love.

I know the pang of deep depression, the frustration of medication side effects, and the stigma that society places on people who have been diagnosed with a mental illness. I have now found my passion, and it's using my experience to help others find healing within themselves. Whether it's domestic violence or mental illness, we all deserve to be safe, respected and encouraged.

I stayed in Flagstaff from 2007-2011 and spent those four years with another man I loved. Although our relationship came to an end, it was one more mountain I was able to climb and come out on the other side as a better person.

If I can survive the devastation of a mental illness, I can survive a heart ache. But I had to rely on what I know works for me. I had to take care of myself and reach out to systems of support. After living with him for four years, the breakup rocked my world. While I made the decision to end it for good, much pain and sadness followed.

After a great deal of love and support from family and friends, in October 2011, I packed up my house and moved to Phoenix. I am now living in a beautiful condo on my own. ON MY OWN! Can you believe a bipolar-ridden, ex-puking, heartbroken girl could do it on her own? Wooo-hoo!

For the last year and a half, I have worked for a statewide domestic violence coalition, where I travel the state of Arizona and provide training for agencies and service organizations that work with victims and survivors of domestic violence and sexual assault. I absolutely love my job, and I can proudly say that I am capable of doing anything I want. Bring it on.

10 FOR US PILL POPPERS

How did I get from there to here in the last many years? How have I managed to have a Serious Mental Illness and still maintain and full life? Well, it didn't happen overnight that's for sure. But I think that having a mental illness has opened my eyes to what the world has to offer and what I'm capable of doing.

I've been through experiences I thought would capsize my life, yet because of them I have grown immeasurably. My strength, faith and ability have all been tested, and I have grown to love the strength I find within myself. Want to know the biggest step to accepting my disorder and maintaining health and stability? MEDICATION.

I just had to face the fact that I would need to take medication, every day, til death do us part. I know it's not ideal; however the damage caused by being off my medication has taken away my freedom, my happiness, my success, and my stability.

I want, need, and deserve quality of life and I've found that managing my medication with Dr. Caspian is step one. I have taken medication every single day since I was released from the hospital in 2002. If you're reading this book, and you're the person seeking support, here are a few suggestions…

The first thing to do is to find a good psychiatrist. What do I mean by good? Someone that makes you feel comfortable and cares about building a rapport with you, beyond your diagnosis. How are they going to know how to get you back on the right track, if they don't know anything about the track your looking to get back on?!

Talk to them about your memories, your interests, and hobbies…the things in your life and bring you purpose and joy. And if you aren't able to recall those positive things, that's okay. Time will change that.

Find someone that you trust, and who allows you to take an active role in your own treatment. You're the only one who knows what you feel like, so your thoughts and input should be heard with great importance. Having a psychiatrist that actively listens to all of your needs is key. If you are not able to be completely open and honest, you are wasting your time and money.

This is YOUR time to be an open book in an environment that is supportive and keeps your best interest at the forefront. Granted, it will take some time to build that rapport, but if you find yourself dreading going to the doctor, or feeling uncomfortable while you're there, find someone new.

It's also nice to remember that you don't always have to talk about meds, mania, side effects or depression when you see your psychiatrist. Focus on other aspects of your life.

When things in your life are going well, your doctor should be thrilled. If the two of you have nothing to talk about unless you are in the midst of a trauma, that should be a red flag.

It's important for them to know who you really are as a person, aside from your diagnosis. Plus, it's not particularly fun only discussing the bad stuff. True, the ugly issues need to be addressed, but growth is found when you explore your true self and what makes you happy.

It may be difficult to remember, but keep searching for things that bring any amount of light into your life. Be in charge of what type of medication you take, how much and how often. Obviously, the psychiatrist is the expert; however they are not the ones taking the pills. Ask questions.

If they recommend you begin taking Effexor, or Abilify, or whatever, find out what need that medication will meet. Is it to treat depression or anxiety? Is it an anti-psychotic? What does anti-psychotic mean? How will it make you feel? Which chemicals in your brain are being affected?

Find out what the side effects are, and do the benefits of the medication outweigh the side effects? What do you do if you experience side effects? Ask what you should feel like once you start taking the medication and how long it will take before it starts working.

I have worked with so many women that are taking 10 or more different mental health medications, and have no idea what they are for. We must educate ourselves so that we can make informed decisions about our medication management. Another "must do" is taking your medication all the time. Medication is like food for our brain. We need it to function, be healthy and live a successful life.

Without medication, we cannot live the balanced life we are capable of living. If you begin a regimen of medication and begin feeling better, cheers! That means the meds are working, not that you should stop taking them.

Consistency is the key to balancing the chemicals in your brain, so you can feel good each and every day. Many people who continuously struggle with bipolar disorder are not properly managing their medication. Think about the quality of your life when you are taking your meds consistently, compared to when you're not.

There are a ton of different medications that treat symptoms of bipolar, depression and anxiety. If you are taking something that you don't like, just keep shopping. Fortunately, there are lots of options out there.

As you try new medications, or new combinations, just know that you will eventually find the perfect cocktail of drugs. Kick the negative outlook you have on medication. The more you resist, the longer it will take for you to find stability.

Now, I'm not going to preach to you about illegal drugs or drinking, but I do have to mention it. The contents of drugs and alcohol drastically change your brain chemistry, specifically when mixed with medication used to treat bipolar. The medication cannot properly do its job, if we are continuously changing its content by adding depressants or stimulants.

While I am not a drug user, I do like to let loose and drink, so I have to be very careful. I've found that a hangover can be the beginning of depression or increase my level of anxiety. It would be ideal if I quit drinking completely; however I would be lying if I said that's on my list of to-do's. So I just have to manage my intake and stay alert with how it might interact with my medication.

It's your call how you chose to live your life, but other than the obvious reasons not to do drugs, you will not be able to manage your bipolar disorder if you are using substances regularly.

I know that some people enjoy the natural high they get when they are manic, which is why they choose not to take medication. And it's true; the high feels like you're on top of the world. But think about how that high affects your life overall.

Are you really able to connect with family and friends, keep a job, attend classes, and tend to relationships? Do you make decisions that damage your life? Get you in legal or financial trouble? Is it really worth it?

Be patient. Know that some medications take weeks, if not months until they are totally disbursed throughout your system. I wish there was a pill we could take that kicked in right when we wanted it to, and although there are fast acting medications, they usually take time.

I've taken different combinations of Lamictal, Celexa, Zyprexa, Haldol, Depakote, Xanax, Wellbutrin and Cymbalta throughout my life, so I know how to fill up a Monday through Friday pill organizer fairly quickly. I don't love the idea that I take this medication, but I know that if I want to have a healthy state of mind and live the life I've worked hard for, I have to take it every day.

Don't shy away from taking your medications because you don't want anyone else to know. It's your decision who you share that with. You're not wearing a sign around your neck that says, "I take antipsychotic meds." It's like the size of your jeans. Nobody else has to know that number, the important part is that they fit you. Same goes with medication.

If there are people in your life that will judge you or treat you differently because you are taking medication, tell them to kick rocks! They are not supportive friends and there is no need for their negativity in your life. We aren't embarrassed to take vitamins, and we shouldn't be embarrassed to take anti-depressants. They both help us stay healthy.

When working with a psychiatrist, the goal is to feel a sense of empowerment. Not that many of the sessions won't be difficult, but you should walk out of that office with tools to better your current situation.

You should feel as though you are gaining insight, support and suggestions so that you can be your own advocate in managing your disorder. It's nice to receive validation that you truly are a strong and capable person, who is able to make informed decisions in your own life.

11 BUMPS IN THE ROAD

I've had two major episodes, one in August of 2001 and the other in August of 2002. Since then, I have not been hospitalized nor had an episode that was anything near the magnitude of the previous ones. With that being said, it has not been all smooth sailing for the last twelve years.

I have changed medications, had emergency visits and phone calls with Dr. Caspian and had to take time off of work or school. I've come to realize that while I can go months, if not years without having any serious issues, there are always going to be bumps in the road.

I actually had the onset of an episode within the last year. I had been feeling a little off for the last few days; nonetheless I continued working and going about my usual routine.

I was in Tucson facilitating a domestic violence training to a group of border patrol officers. Throughout the training, I continuously had onsets of anxiety. I felt as if I couldn't really grasp onto reality in the way that I felt like I was actually in my body. It was a bit like when you're day dreaming and then you come back to reality. Well, I couldn't seem to come back.

While driving back to Phoenix after the training, I felt sick, as if I were high on something I had not taken. Again, some people really like that feeling, but I know how detrimental it is to my life, so any sign of mania causes me to panic.

Journal

February 24th, 2012

I'm flighty. I hate the way this feels, and I haven't felt this way in years. Where am I? Where is my mind? I feel so disconnected; I think I might be dreaming. My thoughts continue over and over and around again. They make no sense at all. I'm constantly anxious, like I have this impending feeling of complete doom.

It feels like my head isn't attached and I don't have the sense of being where I really am. I'm on autopilot. Yeah, I physically know where I am, but I can't feel it. It's like a new place I've never been, and I have no sense of grounding.

I can't feel my feet under my body or the ground beneath my feet. I get the sense that something terrible is going to happen and this mania will land me in the hospital.

I know that I will never go down that wicked path of hospitalization that I have in the past. But it's like déjà vu, and it makes me worry. What if the med changes don't work and I feel like this forever? I hate Zyprexa. I gained 30 pounds the last time I was on it and I dread having the feeling of a heavy heart in the morning. But I know that it works.

It has been so long since I've had an episode, so why now? Please don't take away everything I've worked so hard for. Please don't take over. I'm on Lamictal, Zyprexa and Celexa, and this drugged up feeling is so unfamiliar, it's been so long.

But here it is, my eyes are drooping and my head is spinning. It's going to be alright though; I know this is only temporary. Dr. Caspian has reminded me of that for years. I won't feel like this forever, and I will not let this take over me.

So what do we do in these types of situations? How do we handle the bumps so they don't become road blocks? Recognize the symptoms of having an episode! The sooner you can tell you are having an episode, the earlier you can do something about it.

You might have symptoms of depression, where you have no interest in doing anything, you sleep all day or you have such a deep level of sadness you struggle keeping your head above water.

Or you might experience signs of mania, where you are grandiose, talk constantly, feel a sense of high or stop sleeping. The warning signs of an episode are different for everyone, so the best thing you can do is identify yours.

Was this bump in the road scary for me? Absolutely. My bipolar disorder doesn't care about how strong I am, or how successful I'm doing, it sometimes has a way of creeping up on me.

Even though it has been years without a major episode, this was another reminder that I will always be bipolar. It's not going away, so I have to do my very best to roll with the punches and handle it in the best way I know how.

So how did I avoid a major episode that could have spiraled downward, taking me with it? I recognized the signs of an episode. That doesn't mean I didn't feel scared and frustrated. I felt like saying, *Eat shit bipolar! I'm doing so well, don't do this to me now you bastard!* So I had to practice what I preach...talk with my doctor, adjust my medication, reach out to my systems of support and practice self care.

I immediately called Dr. Caspian and left a message on her machine that I was at the beginning stages of an episode. I then called my parents. I let them know where I was, since I was driving.

I don't recommend driving on the freeway if you're in the middle of an episode, but I was confident that I was catching it early. I declined my parents offer to drive to meet me, and was able to drive the rest of the way to their house.

I talked to them on the phone, and they walked me through every minute of that drive. They validated that I would be okay, and just hearing their voices helped calm me and keep me in the present. I practiced deep breathing.

Now I know I harped on Dr. Reed's "breathing theory," but when you're in a state of crisis, breathing is really important. Dr. Caspian taught me the 8-4-4 method...take a deep breath in for 8 seconds, hold it for 4, and breath out for 4. It works every time.

Within the hour, I received a call back from her. I told her how I was feeling and shared my fears of having another episode. She reassured me that I would not have another episode like I had in the past, because I was medicated.

Obviously my meds needed adjusting, but previously I had an un-medicated brain. I took comfort in knowing these symptoms would be much more manageable since I have been medicated for the last twelve years.

She and I came up with a game plan. Together. I gave input and she made recommendations. We decided that I would increase my Lamictal and she would put me back on Zyprexa. My parents held my hand as I immediately began to cry into the phone. I knew that it was the best decision, as Zyprexa helps bring me down from mania almost immediately; however, I always struggle with weight gain.

I ended up taking a few days off work and stayed at my parent's house here in Phoenix. It took a few days for me to get adjusted to the new levels of medications, but soon I felt better. I avoided what could have been a rollover accident by advocating for myself when I felt things were going astray. A flat tire is an episode from which it is much easier to recover from.

Let's talk about systems of support. I realize that not everyone has family and friends to reach out to, but that doesn't mean you don't have systems of support. Support can be from anyone that brings you comfort, strength and guidance. Reach out to teachers, co-workers, partners, support groups, counseling or religious groups.

Figure out who brings light into your day so that when you have a bump in the road, you can rely on your various forms of support to help you. Who can you be completely broken, vulnerable, and weak in front of? Those kinds of people are the ones that will stick with you when times are tough. You deserve to be brutally honest with what you are feeling and thinking.

Unfortunately, funding resources for mental health services are diminishing every day, which leaves a lot of deserving people feeling alone in the world. It is imperative for those of us who struggle with a mental illness to stand up and encourage systems to continue offering mental health services.

We also must become our own advocates and know that most of our own healing and well being is self-guided. Let's open up the conversation about mental illness and encourage it to be discussed publicly in a manner that doesn't shame or discriminate.

12 SPILLING THE BEANS

Telling someone that you have a mental illness can be, well….scary. After years of living with bipolar disorder, I still find myself in positions where I hesitate. I hesitate sharing my diagnosis; saying those words, letting it out. I fear the electricity in the room will change, and the light in which that person sees me may dim or burn out.

Sure, I typically stand strong and thrive in the face of challenge. But then it happens; I hesitate. I hold back. So how do I move beyond this? How do I find my voice again? I use this as a beautiful reminder that growth is standing just a shallow step beneath that fear. This is where courage is reborn.

My suggestion for sharing your experiences? Spill the beans. You deserve the freedom and empowerment that comes along with it. Remember, regardless of how the other person reacts, YOU have incredible courage. That courage will continue to blossom and grow and you'll find a place within yourself where you're authentically proud of how far you've come. Hold on to that place and visit it often.

When you're opening up about any type of mental health issue, prepare to do some myth busting. It's no secret that some people have very little (accurate) information about mental illness. This in and of itself isn't necessary a problem. However, it is problematic when they've been the disadvantaged recipients of societal stigmas, biases, and untruths.

When people don't have a reliable source to learn about mental illness from, it is understandable that they may buy into these myths and stereotypes. This not only stigmatizes those of us living with a mental illness, but it allows fear to thrive and this shuts out the space needed to talk honestly and openly about mental health.

Use this as an opportunity. Take advantage of their lack of knowledge and provide awareness and education so they can hop over the fence into the yard of understanding and acceptance.

Remember that you are the author of your experiences. There is no need to regurgitate every high, low, and in between that you've experienced while you're sharing appetizers over dinner. The blessing in sharing your story is that it is ALL YOURS.

At whatever pace you are comfortable with, you can unveil the pieces of your life without rush or pressure. I find that spilling the beans in a cliffs note format opens the door for the other person to get involved. They can ask questions. They can validate. They can learn.

Their response is a true indication of whether this person wants to be invested in your life and support you in the future.

Realize that it can be triggering or re-traumatizing for you. Digging back through the pain and tragedy of your life is often painful. Reliving upsetting memories can send you back to that exact place and time. The feelings, the smells, the sounds become real again, and the emotions associated with those moments may return.

This can be avoided when you think through what you want to share before you open your mouth. What topics are off limits? Do you feel emotionally safe reliving these experiences? Are you able to recognize when discussing your illness feels too heavy and it's time to put down the weights?

Take care of yourself afterwards. Self care, self care, self care. This is an active, ongoing process of taking care of yourself emotionally, physically, mentally, and spiritually. You don't step on a treadmill and sprint like a maniac without stretching. You warm up your muscles.

Once you've completed your sweat session, you give yourself time to cool down. You're kind to your body because you've put it through something strenuous. Treat your mind the same way.

Spend time afterwards doing something that calms or fulfills you. Process your experience with a friend, take a nap, read a book, get outdoors…relax. Set up a plan of the people or activities in your life that will offer support once you've spilled the beans. This is your Jacuzzi after putting in miles on the treadmill.

Expect the unexpected. After you discuss your mental illness with someone, they could laugh. They could walk away. They could judge. They could do nothing. I always feared that if I told someone, that person wouldn't take me seriously anymore, or they'd no longer respect me.

Personally, the "do nothing" response has been incredibly painful for me. This fear was born after I spent months with my psychiatrist "preparing my speech" for when I finally opened up to my high school best friends after I'd spent a week in a psychiatric hospital.

My trembling voice carried words that were humiliating as I went over the script of what I felt comfortable sharing. As for them? They stared. Remember that?

They said nothing…and did nothing. So as we prepare to openly talk to family, friends, employers, or new partners, we are doing ourselves a favor if we recognize that they might not respond in the way that we need or hope for.

I once began sharing why I was taking medication to a boyfriend, and with some obvious nervousness in my voice, I told him that it had to do with mental illness. His response was, "well, as long as you're not bipolar, because that would really freak me out." Oh shit.

I literally thought I was going to die. I completely denied being bipolar and said "oh no, it's nothing like that." I was humiliated. But not as much as he was when I finally spilled the beans. Foot. In. Mouth!

Dr. Caspian put it beautifully. She explained to me long ago that not everyone is in a place in their life where they are able to extend the compassion needed to deal with a mental illness. Due to a variety of reasons, some people are not able to give forth any attention or understanding to others in need. They are just not built that way.

It's not necessarily their intent to be inconsiderate or cold, but dealing with crisis or difficult situations is something they simply do not discuss. Her words helped me gain clarity into why I wasn't receiving the support I so greatly desired.

She also helped me recognize that I was effortlessly reaching out for the support of others. The need for validation and acceptance is completely normal. However, it wasn't long before I realized that *I* needed to become comfortable with my diagnosis.

I still had a lot of growing to do. I began to see how important it was for me to find strength from within, rather than to seek out other people's approval. I had no control over how they responded, so I set my focus on looking inward.

When I went back to college my sophomore year and met the girls who continue to play a major part in my life, I found the approval I had always desired. They were my closest friends and over the course of the first semester, they had gotten to know the real Erin Callinan. Not "Erin Callinan, that girl who's bipolar." They loved me for me.

The girls knew that I took medication, but I hadn't exactly been forthcoming about what for. I decided it was time. I was feeling healthy, I was feeling appreciated and I put my trust in them that once I spilled the beans, they wouldn't love me any less.

So I did it. I sat down with Kerry and Kelsey, and I dropped the bomb. And just as I had suspected, they were wonderful! They asked me a bunch of different questions about what it was like, and gave me praise for being able to share such a difficult experience.

They commended me for all my hard work. I felt on top of the world. They even asked what I needed from them to continue living a healthy life. Imagine that!

I explained the different warning signs and indications that things were going astray. I also told them about what triggers me. They knew that I couldn't go without a good night's sleep, hangovers made me anxious, and if I started talking nutty, to call my parents or my brother. They had cell phone numbers for all of them.

It was so refreshing to have friends in my life who accepted me and all my secrets. They gave me the confidence to let those secrets out, and once I did, they no longer carried power over me.

I have dropped the bomb on every guy I have dated since I was 17. None of them broke up with me, nor kick me in the shins and run for the hills. Sure, the boyfriend I mentioned above didn't respond in the most supportive way possible, however, I finally shared the truth with him…and the next four years.

Most people have respected my honesty and are proud of me. To have people that are proud of you, in addition to being proud of yourself feels pretty amazing.

I have disclosed being bipolar to my current employer, as well as my former employer at the domestic violence shelter. Did I share it with everyone at my agency? No way. But in order to really take care of myself, I have needed to take time off of work here and there.

Whether it's because I'm going through medication changes, or had to drive to Flagstaff to see Dr. Caspian, I felt it was important to let them know what I was dealing with. (And yes, I still see Dr. Caspian to this very day! Twelve years strong, baby!)

Both of my employers have been tremendously supportive, and respected my privacy and shared nothing with other staff members. Employers are required to maintain confidentiality regarding medical concerns, so advocate for yourself and know that all information you share should remain confidential.

As you move forward in your spilling the beans journey, be prepared for the "I have a friend" response. Guess what? Mental illness is incredibly common! I cannot begin to count how many times people have responded to my experiences with, "my brother, my wife, my best friend, etc."

This is great news! Not only have you opened the door for continued conversation, but you're connecting yourself to other people who also live with a mental illness. It is really powerful to be able to talk to other people with similar experiences. It makes you feel less alone.

You can be a beacon of hope to others who may still be struggling. You have taken the lead and shown that mental illness isn't the driver of your life. You're sitting tall behind the wheel, seat belt securely fastened, with bright eyes on the exciting road ahead.

13 NOURISH YOUR SOUL

As you learn to take care of yourself, it's important to know the difference between self comfort and self care. Self comfort is when we do something that gives us instant gratification. This doesn't necessarily nourish your soul, but it eases the current situation nonetheless.

For example, when I am stressed out I like to delight in margaritas on the rocks with salt. Pair that with chips, salsa and queso dip...delicious!

Is this activity something that is taking care of my body physically, emotionally, spiritually and mentally? That would be a negative. We all practice self comfort from time to time, and that's okay. Whether it be drinking, smoking, eating, or spending money, these things can assist in getting us through that initial moment.

We want to avoid using self comfort as the only form of taking care of ourselves. We want to practice self care on a daily basis. Self care is anything you do to nourish your soul which promotes physical, emotional, spiritual, and mental well being. There are many forms of self care, and you can develop your own routine of what works for you.

If self care is a newer concept for you, here are some examples to get you started. Self care can be hiking, yoga, art, meditation, crafts, exercise, prayer, reading, sports, writing, listening to music, riding a bike, sleeping, or spending time with family or friends. Just to name a few!

Anything you can identify that keeps you grounded and is healthy for you long term is a wonderful form of self care. I have found that laughter is one of the greatest ways to nourish my soul. Laughter can be a great coping mechanism to help get us through the tough times. Yes, it's important to address our real emotions and feelings, but why can't we laugh at ourselves a little?

Life is full of serious issues and tragedies, and if we aren't able to find some form of humor in our own lives, finding healing, especially with a mental illness can be much more difficult. Did I laugh when I was in the hospital, or once I got out and experienced a great deal of depression? Definitely not.

But as I began to stabilize and get back on my feet, my sense of humor returned. Try your best to spend time with people who make you laugh. I'm talking deep down, belly laughs that bring tears to your eyes. That's nourishing your soul.

Are there people in your life who bring about negativity and don't practice a healthy life style themselves? Do they criticize you for the ups and downs you've had, or fail to give you any type of positive support? Do they drag you down, instead of build you up? I'm sure you have at least one person like that in your life. I know I did.

It's going to be difficult, but if you want to truly live a stable and healthy life, you must surround yourself with other people who are stable and healthy. Does that mean that you have to cut ties with anybody who doesn't spend their time meditating and reading self help books? No.

But the less negativity you have in your life, the greater the chances are that positive things will come into your life. Surrounding yourself with people that you can depend on, who love you unconditionally and provide support when you need it the most can greatly increase your chances of managing your disorder in a healthy way.

These are people who you can share your heart with and express the many ways bipolar disorder has affected your life. They can be on your team and support you in managing your meds and practicing self care. These people don't run away when there are bumps in the road, they stand by your side and help you through your most vulnerable times.

Choosing to have healthy people share in your journey of life is a wonderful indication that you are being proactive and practicing good self care. Be incredibly proud of that. Embrace your creativity.

This can be a huge release when dealing with stress. I love the idea of being able to see the progression of something I've created, and gaining the satisfaction of the final product. You don't need to be an expert to get creative and have some fun. Try photography, knitting, watercolor, beading, or poetry. Whatever floats your boat!

As you move forward in your own recovery, remember that we didn't choose to be bipolar anymore than someone chooses to have cancer. It just doesn't work that way. It doesn't determine who I am or what I am capable of doing. I simply won't allow it to. You don't have to either. If you are in the early stages of a diagnosis, I know how difficult it is to take a blow like that.

Even in the words I used throughout this book as I described my experiences...crazy, looney bin, mental, lunatic. Those were words that I really thought applied to me. If I made a bit of humor out of them, I would feel more "normal."

But over time, I've realized the damage that can cause, and those are words I try to get others to STOP using to describe people with a mental illness. They only feed the stigma that those who are SMI stand no chance of living a life that others without a mental illness have access to.

So find the difference between trying to make sense of your disorder, and using negative self talk that makes you feel less than.

Give yourself time. Allow yourself the freedom to process how you are feeling. It's okay to feel sad, frustrated, scared, angry or confused. You might experience all of the above. As you are able to make sense of what bipolar disorder is, you'll begin to make progress down the path toward improvement.

How do we improve our thinking about having a mental illness? Educate yourself. Education literally saved me and my family. Learn everything you can about bipolar disorder. The more tools you arm yourself with, the easier it will be to manage future bumps in the road.

You should have seen the bookshelves at my parent's house. It was like a psychiatrist's office, yet with titles like, "Bipolar Disorder for Dummies."

Here's my disclaimer: much of what you read in the news or online may not be positive. You will come across horrific stories and devastation left behind due to the actions of someone who suffers from bipolar disorder.

The reality is that there are people out there who cause harm and do not take responsibility for managing their own disorder. Let's not be one of those people. We only have to "suffer" from bipolar if we choose to.

Do not be discouraged when you reach out for further education and you are faced with disappointment, blame or judgment. Keep on reading. There are plenty of great websites, publications and books out there, along with millions of advocates who cheer on people with mental illnesses.

Encourage your family to do their own research as well. The more people you have on your team, understanding the effects of bipolar, the better. We want to remember that our disorder is not only difficult for us, but it can be just as hard for our friends and family.

UPS must have shown up at my parents' doorstep every week for years. The combination of their amazing hearts and desire to educate themselves about my disorder allowed us to grow together as a family.

It's also important that we address the stigma surrounding mental illness. It's there, and we can't pretend it's not. But that doesn't mean we must allow the stigma to silence us. Once you are comfortable with your diagnosis, you might get to a place where you also can openly talk about it. What happens when we speak out about our mental illness? What happens when we spill the beans to people outside of our family and friends?

We are showing others that it's okay to be living bipolar disorder and there is nothing to be ashamed of. We are also giving them permission to talk about mental illness in a new light. Together, we can serve as role models and illustrate that people who are bipolar can live completely normal and functional lives.

Standing up and speaking out against the stigma is also providing validation to others who might be suffering. It might encourage someone else to talk about their situation once they've seen that we did it, and didn't lose any appendages along the way.

Nobody has ever spit in my face or called the police when I spoke about my mental illness. You may choose to never speak about being bipolar, and that is absolutely your prerogative.

It doesn't mean that you are embarrassed, or don't care about breaking the stigma of mental illness. Every person must decide what is best for them, and be mindful of their own situation.

If you are reading this book, you are already part of the solution. You are choosing to acknowledge that you have been faced with challenges, but are not going to let them ruin your life. I commend you for having the strength to reach out and seek guidance through the experience of another.

I promise you can get through this. It's not going to be easy, and there might be difficulties along the way. Thankfully though, bipolar disorder is treatable! You deserve to be happy and healthy, and I know I do too. So nourish your soul along the way and hold your head up high.

ABOUT THE AUTHOR

Erin Callinan was born in 1984 and grew up in Flagstaff, AZ. She attended Sinagua High School and later moved to Tucson, AZ to attend the University of Arizona, where she graduated with her Bachelor of Arts in Elementary Education. Since 2008, Erin Callinan has dedicated her life to working with victims and survivors of sexual and domestic violence. She has lived in Phoenix since 2011 and travels throughout the country and state of Arizona providing education, training and awareness. Erin joined several mental health organizations and began speaking out about her experiences of living with a mental illness as a means to shatter the stigma surrounding it. She is a highly passionate individual and determined to focus her time and energy to making a positive impact in the world.

Erin Callinan may be reached at:
erin@beautifullybipolar.com
www.beautifullybipolar.com

ERIN CALLINAN

Made in the USA
Columbia, SC
26 July 2020